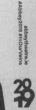

FUNDED BY THE ARTS COUNCIL OF IRELAND

24 HOURS 7 DAYS A WEEK

DOUGLAS HYDE GALLERY

2019

Exhibition Runs →

FREE GARRETT PHELAN

THOUGHT

FM

BROADCASTING 25th MARCH - 23rd APRIL 2019

11th

14th MARCH - 18th MAY 2019

COVER VERSION

A WORK OF ART

ON LINE

LIVE RADIO PERFORMANCE

pre-recorded programming also

No Room For Subtlety

EQUAL

ACCESS

TO EDUCATION

AND

OPPORTUNITY

GHT CLASS DISCRIMINATION

PUBLIC FUNDING USED TO SUPPORT WHO NEEDS IT MOST

THERE ARE BETTER WAYS. EDUCATION, CLASS AND FREE THOUGHT FM

GARRETT PHELAN
→ The Douglas Hyde Gallery
of Contemporary Art

CONTENTS

INTRODUCTION

→ Georgina Jackson

Director, The Douglas Hyde Gallery of Contemporary Art

Garrett Phelan's multi-faceted project *FREE THOUGHT FM* began with a question: how can things be different? This question arose while working on a previous artwork, *HEED FM*, in which Phelan had many conversations with young Dubliners about the things they were passionate about. He also witnessed up close a system that prevents young people from achieving their aspirations and dreams. During this process, there were two barriers that kept coming up again and again: access to education and class inequality.

What began in the extended conversations of *HEED FM* grew over time into the *FREE THOUGHT FM* project, an ambitious and unique artwork involving many people that mobilised the radio waves as an immediate and urgent public space. People were brought together to talk at length, to tease out problems, to amplify their stories and to delve into possible solutions to a system that breeds inequality.

FREE THOUGHT FM was a 30-day live radio broadcast across the city of Dublin, and online. Students, artists, academics, community groups, activists and many others spoke with Phelan and hosts Shane Brothwood, David Joyce, Calvin Darcy-Kanda, Tamara Harawa, Michelle Kinsella and Sophie Mullervey, about their own experiences of education live from the Douglas Hyde located on the campus of Trinity College Dublin.

These live conversations formed the core of FREE THOUGHT FM, and their vibrancy and concerns were amplified through different media: an installation of Phelan's drawings in vinyl and paint across the walls of the gallery, which remained open to visitors beyond the conclusion of the live radio broadcast; a youth-focused marketing campaign to build awareness of diverse routes to education and the support systems available, on billboards across the city and online through social media; a booklet with further details on routes and supports for education distributed online as a PDF, and in print at the gallery and to schools in Dublin; a series of talks in schools with artists, sports people and politicians, speaking about their own experiences of education; and finally, this book.

Rather than simply mapping the project, this book invites key guests, including geographer Gerry Kearns, educator Kathleen Lynch, secondary school principal Liam Wegimont and architectural historian Ellen Rowley, to expand upon the issues that most concern them: how class and education has shaped, and continues to limit, exclude and prohibit, young people and adults' fulfilment and futures.

To begin, Kathleen Lynch explores the role that education plays in our economically stratified society in the reproduction of the class system, where "privilege is enabled to perpetuate itself". But crucially, she highlights the potential of education to break this chain. As she remarks, "[e]ducation has great potential to generate new ways of thinking, knowing and seeing the world if it is enabled and facilitated to exercise its own power".[1] With over 25 years in secondary education in Ireland, Liam Wegimont rings the alarm bells and demands the abolition of the final secondary school exam, the Leaving Certificate. As he states, "[it] is the single biggest obstacle within the Irish education system to the improvement of that system; an impediment to teaching, to learning, to care, to well-being, to community, to student flourishing and to joy".[2] Gerry Kearns looks at the divisions within Dublin, stating, "[t]here is nothing casual about the social geography of Dublin. It has always been inherently political".[3] In tracing how these lines have been drawn, Kearns also looks at how divisions persist, proposing that a very different Dublin is needed. Ellen Rowley steps into the space of the home, thinking through the continuous entanglement of class, housing and difference, from the monopoly of the Irish suburban house to inner-city tenement flats. As she emphasises, "[s]ocial stratification and housing history are long-term bedfellows".[4]

Delving into FREE THOUGHT FM, Rachel O'Dwyer considers Phelan's longstanding use of radio alongside its history as "an idealised public space", as well as reflecting on transmission and sound waves themselves. Exploring the power dynamics in radio she notes, "[a]s with his interest in exclusion and access in education, Phelan is also interested... in who gets to speak and have a voice, in what is represented and what is omitted".[5]

In our conversation, Garrett and I think through the generation of the project and its many facets, what we learned and next steps. Finally, looking back on the project, artist Sarah Pierce acknowledges how "we enter a whole rubric of grammars, systems and structures that represent the work and affect how it behaves and is received – archive, exhibition, broadcast, publicity and information. *FREE THOUGHT FM* is all of this at once".[6] She reflects on access and equality of knowledge, recognising that we are all agents of change.

This book would not have been possible without the passion and trust of many individuals: Garrett for his creativity and commitment in realising a groundbreaking artwork as well as everyone who contributed to its realisation; Gerry Kearns, Kathleen Lynch, Rachel O'Dwyer, Sarah Pierce, Ellen Rowley and Liam Wegimont for their stirring explorations of class, education, geography, architecture, communication, community and the possibilities of art; the amazing team and board at the Douglas Hyde; Rachel Donnelly for her intelligence and keen eye; Noelle Cooper at Unthink for her inventiveness and skill in making this book what you hold in your hands; and to The Arts Council | An Chomhairle Ealaíon for their visionary *Making Great Artwork Open Call* award.

FREE THOUGHT FM began with a question and amassed many answers. A key question that remains is how to change a system so embedded within society that it operates in the realm of 'the social' – taken for granted and obscured through its pervasiveness. There is urgent work to be done and we are all the agents of that change. There are always better ways.

Endnotes

1.   Lynch, K. (2021). Social Class Inequality in Ireland: What Role Does Education Play? In Phelan, G. (ed.) *There Are Better Ways: Education, Class and* FREE THOUGHT FM, p. 37.

2.   Wegimont, L. (2021). Free Thought, Education for Social Change and the Need for Educational Reform. In Phelan, G. (ed.) *There Are Better Ways: Education, Class and* FREE THOUGHT FM, p. 50.

3.   Kearns, G. (2021). Sorting the City. In Phelan, G. (ed.) *There Are Better Ways: Education, Class and* FREE THOUGHT FM, p. 59.

4.   Rowley, E. Back to the Flats: Housing and Class – Architectures, Novels and Lodgers. In Phelan, G. (ed.) *There Are Better Ways: Education, Class and* FREE THOUGHT FM, p. 76.

5.   O'Dwyer, R. 105.2FM: 'this conversation is an artwork'. In Phelan, G. (ed.) *There Are Better Ways: Education, Class and* FREE THOUGHT FM, p. 100.

6.   Pierce, S. Access at its Most Attentive. Notes on *FREE THOUGHT FM*. In Phelan, G. (ed.) *There Are Better Ways: Education, Class and* FREE THOUGHT FM, p. 138.

FREE
THOUGHT FM

Exhibition:
15 March – 25 May 2019

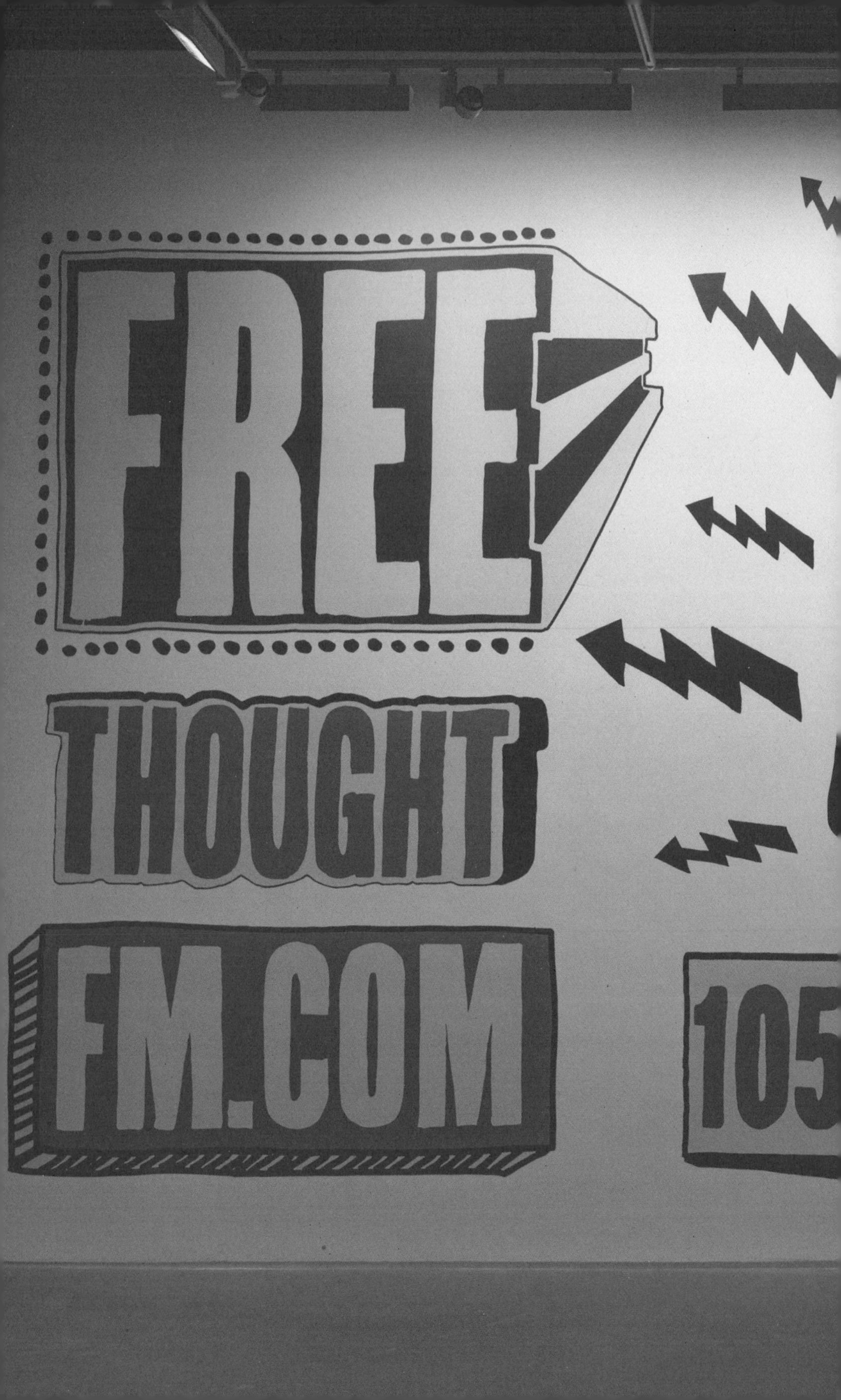
FREE
THOUGHT
FM.COM
105

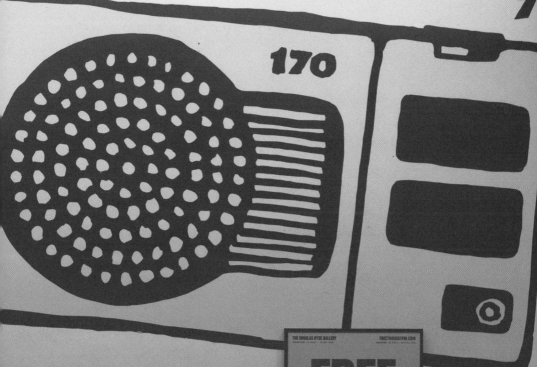

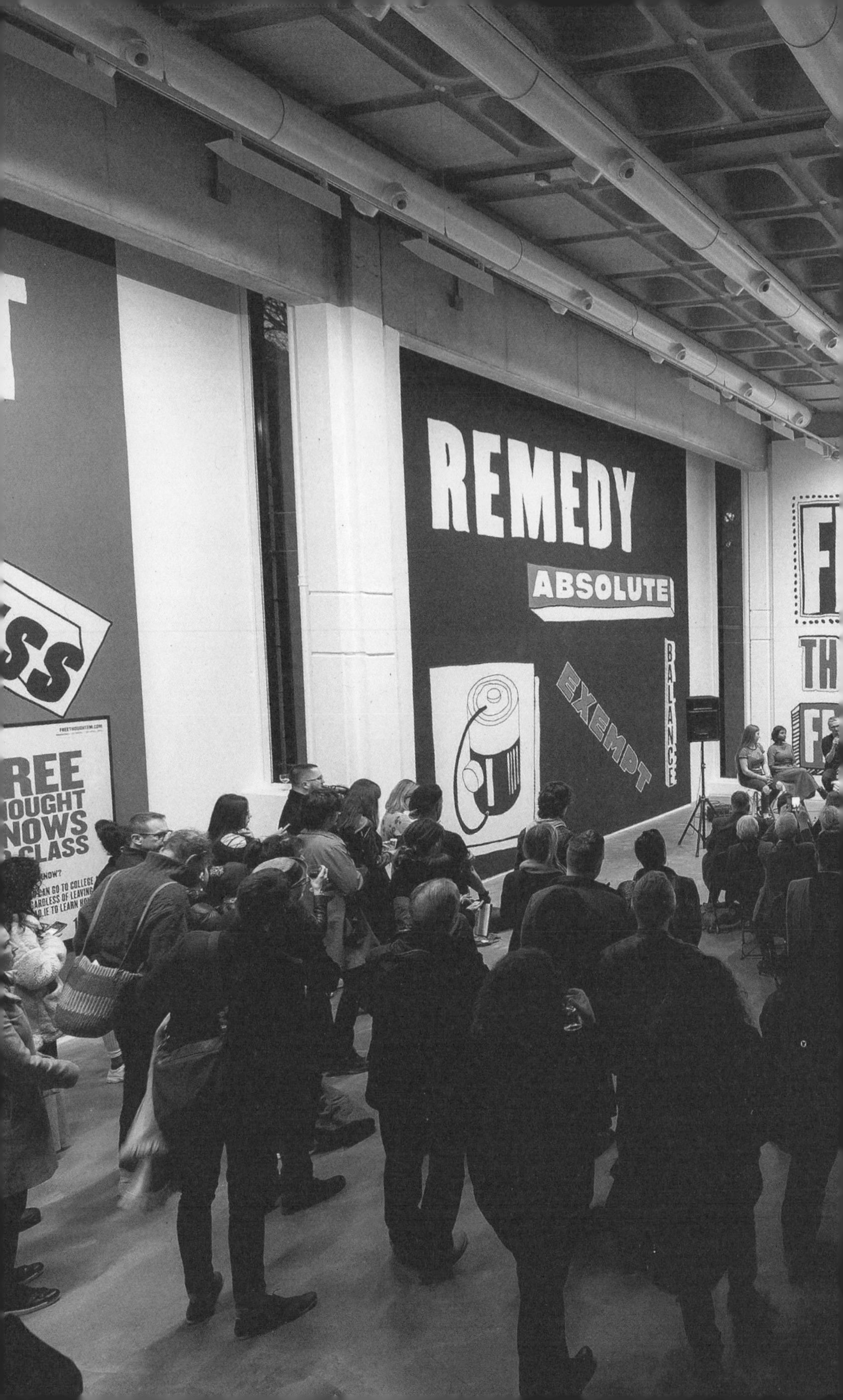
REMEDY
ABSOLUTE
EXEMPT
BALANCE

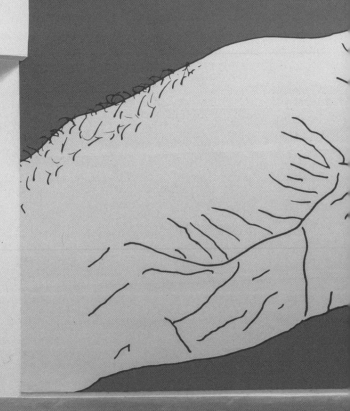

ETUITY

SPHERE

NURTURE

ss

THE DOUGL

EXHIBITION: 15

IF YO

MAT

arts
council
visual

EDUCATION
+ CLASS

SOCIAL CLASS INEQUALITY IN IRELAND: WHAT ROLE DOES EDUCATION PLAY?

- ## Class inequality in Ireland: the overall picture

Since the 1970s, the richest 1%[1] has acquired a rising share of gross income in Ireland, while the share of the remaining 99% has fallen.[2] While the level of income inequality is lower in Ireland than in the UK and USA, it is higher than several of our European neighbours.[3] Ireland relies heavily on social transfers (social welfare and other redistributive mechanisms) to reduce income inequality, as market income inequality, income before taxes and social transfers are all relatively high here.[4]

As the data above does not account for wealth inequalities, it does not show the full picture. Unearned wealth inequalities in Ireland are very high and have been for a long time.[5] This really matters as unearned and inherited wealth remains the main reason why people stay poorer or wealthier from generation to generation.[6]

In Ireland, 72.7% of net wealth is owned by the top 20%, which is higher than the Euro Area average of 67.6%. Only 10% of households own any land,[7] so land ownership is highly concentrated amongst the wealthiest households. The top 20% owns more than 90% of all land (by value), while the top 10% owns 82%.[8]

While statistics such as those outlined above may appear very dry and tedious to read, they have very human and corporeal implications; income and wealth inequalities impact directly on people's quality of life, their life expectancy and their health, both physical and mental.[9] They also have huge impacts on people's experience of education.

- ## Educational inequality

Economic inequality is relational; the wealth of the few comes at a cost to the many. In March 2020, there were almost 1,500 children living in Direct Provision Centres, while a further 3,500 were in homeless accommodation; this data is indicative of the depth of poverty and inequality in Ireland. But it is not the whole picture as social class and, increasingly, racialised inequality have many faces.[10]

The majority of Traveller children still do not complete second-level education, while migrant children are more likely to leave school early than native Irish children, and are disproportionately educated in larger urban schools in the more socio-economically disadvantaged areas.[11] Access to the most selective higher education courses,[12] such as medicine, is heavily dominated by those from the most affluent (white Irish) families.[13][14]

Recognising the persistence of classed inequalities is not to deny that there have been significant improvements in rates of participation and attainment in education for those in lower-income groups over the past two decades. However, what the State does to address injustices with one hand, it frequently undermines with the other.

Privilege is enabled to perpetuate itself. Basic aid is given to those most disadvantaged, but income and wealth inequalities persist; the aid to the most disadvantaged is never adequate to make up the difference. Within education, the most clear-cut and persistent example of this is the continued State funding of socially selective secondary schools, which, on their own admission, set out to educate the elite,[15] thereby perpetuating classed inequality in a systematic way with the support of the State.

- ### Education as a competition for privilege

While being educated is of great personal value, in socio-political terms education is a positional good: its value is always relative to what others have in educational terms. Because there is no equality of condition in an economically unequal society like Ireland, the competition for educational goods (degrees, a good Leaving Certificate etc.) is never a fair one; competitors are unequally resourced going into the competition and those with the most resources are most likely to perform the best.

Resources are not only confined to money; they also include social networks (who you know and don't know).[16] A study involving Ireland and a number of other Western European countries by Maurizio Franzini and Michele Raitano (2013) highlights this point.[17] Even when people have comparable college degrees and grades, the class position of their social origins impacts the prestige and income of the jobs they enter, to the advantage of the already privileged. In other words, class-based social networks contribute to social-class-biased labour market differentials outside of education.

- ### Education and the reproduction of the class system

While inequalities outside of education impact on those within, the internal life of education is not neutral in class terms. Education, or more accurately, the formal education system, is intimately bound up with the reproduction of the class structures of our society.

To begin with, the school system is largely designed, managed and controlled by those who are already the successful beneficiaries of that system, and these tend to be the same people who have power, status and money in other areas of economic, cultural and political life. Those who plan schools, design curricula, and set and assess examinations are generally part of the cultural elite of society. And while the cultural elite (most of whom are middle class or upper middle class) are not necessarily part of the economic elite, there is deep overlap between the owners of wealth and the owners and controllers of cultural and social capital in Ireland and elsewhere.[18][19]

Though the so-called cultural elite can, and do, differentiate themselves from the business elite in taste, lifestyle and how they spend their money, the two are deeply interwoven socially and politically. They exercise control, both individually and collectively, in the definition of 'merit' and 'educational success' (be it in terms of art, music, literature, economics, politics, business, science, technology or social policy), and they always define merit in a way that ensures their own children are meritorious.[20] This is evident in how any attempt to change the rules of the educational game that might undermine the current system of class reproduction is met with staunch and class-mobilised opposition.[21] The successful challenge by a small group of powerful parents and associates in socially selective (fee-paying but State subvented) schools to outlaw selection based on past pupils' attendance, is proof of this.[22]

- ### Education and the reproduction of the class system: are we trying to do the impossible?

Having educational credentials such as degrees and diplomas may suggest these are acquired by hard work and exceptional abilities (namely merit) when in fact their acquisition is strongly conditioned by social class positioning in Ireland and elsewhere.[23]

Pierre Bourdieu and Jean-Claude Passeron's claims that the true purpose of education is 'social selection under the guise of technical selection', that it is engaged in reproducing social hierarchies by translating them into academic hierarchies,[24] is a challenging but truthful observation. But this sociological reality is glossed over and normalised in Ireland. What has happened is that schools have managed to convince those who are relatively unsuccessful in formal educational terms (such as those in low reading groups, streams or bands, or those doing foundation or ordinary level subjects)[25] that they owe their lowly educational and occupational status 'to their lack of gifts or merit', their lack of so-called intelligence.

The nineteenth century myths of the genetic determinists and eugenicists live residually[26] in the culture of every classroom in Ireland. Teachers believe in the myth of the 'bright' and 'weak' student, thereby exonerating themselves, and society more generally, from having responsibility for children failing in schools.

In other words, through the habit of being failed (not being the star), the perpetually failing students (working class, Travellers, ethnic minorities) believe they are legitimately dispossessed because "...*in matters of culture absolute dispossession excludes awareness of being dispossessed* [my emphasis]".[27] Being dispossessed means one lacks the power, the confidence, the language and/or the means to challenge the dispossession.

Bourdieu and Passeron (1977) dismiss the idea that education can be reformed from within to become emancipatory. They regard attempts at transforming education as a naïve exercise, a utopianism that would not be permitted given the power of those who exercise pedagogic authority.[28] This position is open to question, however. Radical changes have happened in education in the past and they can happen again in the future. What we first must do is recognise where schools can generate change, and where and what they cannot change.[29]

There are many things that educationalists can do, but they cannot change the social class structures of society on their own. The reason for this is that the generative (primary) site of social-class-based injustices is not located within the education system in the first instance.

It was the political shocks arising from wide-scale war that contributed significantly to the reduction of classed inequality in most developed countries between 1910 and 1950.[30] And it was the restructuring of the economies and occupational structures in Western capitalist states in the post WWII period (notably the rise of so-called white-collar jobs) that enabled absolute rates of social mobility to rise, not changes in education *per se*.[31] Contrarily, in the post-1980 period, it was the deregulation and geopolitics of taxation and finance that contributed significantly to the rise of economic inequality.[32]

The rise of precarious work, zero-hour contracts and the proliferation of low-waged economies in the service sector in Western capitalist states[33] is not the direct outcome of actions in the education sector. Education cannot prevent powerful employers creating low-paid jobs, or failing to provide pensions for their workers; it cannot directly alter the structure of the capitalist economy that creates the inequality that contributes to unequal access to, and participation in, education.[34]

The new oligarchic rich are global citizens and increasingly detached from nation states and their policies;[35] *noblesse oblige* does not apply. It is not the educational institutions *per se* that enable them to maintain their class advantage through inheritance, low taxes on wealth, deregulated financial markets and the free movement of capital across borders. The latter is a function of mobilised class power, be it in international law, military spending, fiscal policy, and/ or the legislative and political infrastructures of global capitalist economies. The super-rich can block wealth taxes and buy political majorities through campaign contributions, while maintaining social legitimacy through philanthropy.[36] In determining levels of inequality, "inherited wealth comes close to being as decisive at the beginning of the twenty-first century as it was in the age of Honoré de Balzac's Père Goriot".[37] Major class inequalities are not a product of educational policy *per se*. To the contrary, "the main force in favour of equality has been the diffusion of knowledge and skills".[38]

• **What schools can change: education's emancipatory potential**

While education can and does contribute to classed and racialised inequalities, it is impossible to imagine any serious challenge to these inequalities without education playing its part. Education is not a black box governed only by powerful class interests. Those who work and learn within it have educational and political agency, as feminist scholars such as bell hooks[39][40] have demonstrated. The work of Jacques Rancière[41] and Paulo Freire,[42] and of those who have followed in Freire's educational and policy footsteps,[43] shows that education need not simply be a site of class reproduction.

The power of education to frame social consciousness is proven by the intensity of the political battles that have taken place historically over education. It was evident in colonial times, when education was regarded as an effective means of domesticating local populations,[44] and in the early twenty-first century where it is used as a means of promoting employment-centred education (especially in STEM subjects) by the OECD and the European Commission, through country reports and the Lisbon Agreement respectively. It is also evident in the move by the conservative government in Hungary to close the Central European University in Budapest, and the removal of politically dissenting academics from their posts in Turkey in 2016/2017.

If education were powerless in realising social change, then governments and other powerful interest groups would not try to control it. As many scholars, from Antonio Gramsci to Louis Althusser, and from Freire to Alan Touraine and hooks, have observed, the mind is a site of political struggle, and education is a venue in which power struggles over intellectual and ideological formation take place. Education has great potential to generate new ways of thinking, knowing and seeing the world if it is enabled and facilitated to exercise its own power.

At the interpersonal level, education has liberatory potential if one believes and trusts in the 'equality of intelligences' between students and teachers.[45] Replacing 'stultifying' education with emancipatory education, where the educator recognises the abilities of all people to come to know and learn, has powerful transformative potential. Contrary to what Bourdieu claims, Rancière argues that liberation is possible if education takes place among a 'community of equals' and educators recognise the intellectual capacities of all people.[46] Like Freire (1970), Rancière holds that if radical educational change is to happen there must be a new pedagogy deployed, moving from banking education to critical thinking and engagement.[47] The reality is that "...no party or government, no army, school or institution, will ever emancipate a single person."[48]

Liberatory education is about the educational relationship itself.[49] Education can be liberatory when it enables people to trust in their own abilities to come to know the world and to frame it in their own terms. It is possible to abandon 'banking education', where education has become "an act of depositing, in which the students are the depositories and the teacher is the depositor ... [where] the teacher issues communiques and makes deposits which the students patiently receive, memorize, and repeat."[50] Liberatory education begins with the resolution of the teacher-student contradiction, by reconciling the poles of the contradiction so that both are simultaneously teachers and students.

- ## Conclusion

While education institutions alone cannot eliminate social class (or racial) inequalities, as the generative site of social class injustices rests on economic rather than educational relations, what educators can do is challenge the doxas (the unnamed and unspoken underground values) of their own educational trade. They can do this first by calling out, through emancipatory pedagogical practices and new curriculum developments, the internal contradictions of the education system, particularly its classed, raced, dis-ability and gendered contradictions. They can enable students to read the way racial, gender and class power is encoded within educational knowledge and practice, thereby freeing students to rethink it and challenge what is oppressive and unjust.

Educators can challenge the knowledge hierarchies that are institutionalised in schools and colleges whereby certain subjects and forms of knowledge, especially logical-mathematical and scientific knowledge,[51] are deemed superior to artistic, interpersonal, relational and kinaesthetic knowledges, and to critical understanding. Educators can challenge the myth of meritocracy whereby it is wrongly assumed that the educationally successful are the most 'intelligent' (ignoring the fact that there are multiple intelligences rather than one) and the most 'valuable' to society.

Educators could also open a debate about how economic inequality undermines equality in education at every level in Ireland's 'pay-as-you-go' system of supposedly free, but actually unfree, education. From paying for primary school books, to paying for extracurricular activities, to paying for having Leaving Certificate grades re-corrected, Ireland is replete with minor but cumulative classed inequalities. As insiders, teachers and lecturers need to challenge these at every turn. One minor, but simple place to start would be by challenging the practice whereby one has to pay (a lot of money over many years) to learn a musical instrument privately to get the best grades in the performance part of the Leaving Certificate music examination (which now counts for 50% of the total grade).[52] A similar situation applies in relation to Gaeilge. Now that 50% of the Leaving Certificate examination grade is for spoken Irish, those who can afford to pay for their children to attend the Gaeltacht each year[53] are automatically class advantaged. These blatantly class-biased public examination arrangements are not seriously challenged by powerful educational insiders, though they compound class inequalities by enabling students with private funding to get significantly higher grades in public examinations.

As Paulo Freire, bell hooks and Jacques Rancière have observed, education is not neutral nor is it mechanical; teachers have the capacity to be dialogical liberating educators in how they teach, in the curricula they design and in how they assess students. Students can be actively engaged critical learners and partners in this process if enabled to do so. To start this process, teachers must believe in the equality of intelligences of all students, as Rancière and Freire have proposed. It is time that the nineteenth and twentieth century myths about human intelligences were finally laid to rest; it is time to recognise the developmental character of intelligence and the multiple forms it takes.[54]

While schools and places of education have liberatory potential, they are not without class contradictions. They operate as sites for the reproduction of classed inequalities and sites for resistance to these very same injustices conterminously. Yet they can exploit those contradictions to resist injustices when the opportunity arises.[55]

Educators are in a powerful position to exercise agency, including teacher educators, and educators of other professionals. They occupy the role of institutional intellectuals in society; as such, they are potential agents for cultural innovation and critique. Educators have the power to enable and facilitate dissent against injustices, should they choose to exercise that power. And this is not a new phenomenon, as educational institutions have long been at the centre of political movements for egalitarian change, enabling and facilitating resistance to oppression in many different countries.[56] Universities were sites of mobilisation against injustices in Poland during the Second World War: 184 professors from the University of Kraków (Jagiellonian University) were arrested and deported to Sachsenhausen concentration camp for their refusal to comply with Nazi orders. Universities and Centres of Education played a key role in the mobilisation of the American civil rights movement, and, most recently, in mobilising communities in the USA against television advertising to children in schools. However, teachers cannot become and remain critical educators if emancipatory practice and its theory are not a core part of teacher education programmes. For teachers to be liberated, their own education needs to be liberatory rather than mechanistic.[57] Is it? Do teacher education students read and engage with the works of liberatory educators such as Freire, hooks and Rancière today?

Education is potentially liberatory both socially and personally. Teachers, academics and other educators can challenge injustices when they are educated to recognise them and supported and enabled to call them out and address them, individually and collectively. Like all other professionals, teachers also need to reflect on their own class positioning and how it influences their action or lack of action for justice. They need to ask this question: to what extent are we, as professional educators, net beneficiaries and/or enablers of classed injustices, both in our professional and personal lives?

Endnotes

1. Those with incomes over €200,000 involving 18,741 tax cases in 2015.

2. The top 1% earned 4.8% of Ireland's income in 1977, 5.2% in 1986 and 11.5% in 2015. The top 10% earned 23% of Ireland's income in 1977, 26.1% in 1986 and 37.2% in 2015. Available at: https://wid.world/country/ireland/.

3. O'Connor, N. and Staunton, C. (TASC). (2015). *Cherishing All Equally: Economic Inequality in Ireland*. TASC Report. Dublin: TASC, pp. 30–32.

4. Callan et al. (2018). Income growth and income distribution: a long-run view of Irish experience. *Budget Perspectives 2019,* Paper 3. Dublin: ESRI, Economic and Social Research Institute.

5. In 2018, almost 70% of those with the highest net wealth (the top 10%) had received a substantial inheritance or gift compared to one in ten of those with the lowest net wealth (the bottom 10%). *CSO Household Finance and Consumption Survey 2018*. Available at: www.cso.ie/en/releasesandpublications/ ep/p-hfcs/householdfinanceand consumptionsurvey2018/summaryofresults/.

6. Piketty, T. (2014). *Capital in the Twenty-First Century*. Cambridge Mass.: Harvard University Press.

7. That is excluding home ownership, which has traditionally been high in Ireland but has declined steadily since austerity, from 2008 onwards.

8. Staunton, C. (TASC). (2015). *The Distribution of Wealth in Ireland*. Dublin: TASC.

9. Wilkinson, R.G. and Pickett, K. (2009). *The Spirit Level: Why More Equal Societies Almost Always Do Better*. London: Penguin; Wilkinson, R.G. and Pickett, K. (2018). *The Inner Level: How More Equal Societies Reduce Stress, Restore Sanity and Improve Everybody's Wellbeing*. London: Allen Lane (Penguin).

10. The No Child 2020 Irish Times initiative focused on many different inequalities experienced by children from low-income families in Ireland. Available at: https://irishtimes.com/nochild2020.

11. Kitching, K. Racism in education. Irish Network Against Racism. Available at: https://inar.ie/racism-and-education/.

12. These are courses which ultimately lead to high-income jobs in medicine, dentistry, law, financial and actuarial services etc.

13. HEA (Higher Education Authority). (2019). *Higher Education Spatial & Socio-Economic Profile, 2017/18*. Dublin: HEA.

14. While 15% of the second-level school student body is defined as 'disadvantaged', just 10% of the higher education student body is so classified. While 36% of the enrolment in medicine is from the most affluent families in the country (and just 15% of the population is classified as affluent overall), only 3.5% of enrolments in medicine come from 'disadvantaged' backgrounds (ibid.).

15. Courtois, A. (2018). *Elite Schooling and Social Inequality: Privilege and Power in Ireland's Top Private Schools*. Basingstoke: Palgrave Macmillan.

16. Kennedy, M. and Power, M. (2010). The smokescreen of meritocracy: Elite education in Ireland and the reproduction of class privilege. *Journal for Critical Education Policy Studies* 8 (2): pp. 222–248.

17. Frazini, M. and Raitano, M. (2013). Economic inequality and its impact on intergenerational mobility. *Intereconomics* 6: pp. 328–334.

18. Bourdieu, P. and Passeron, J.C. (1977). *Reproduction in Education, Society and Culture*. Beverly Hills: Sage; Courtois, A. (2018). *Elite Schooling and Social Inequality: Privilege and Power in Ireland's Top Private Schools*. Basingstoke: Palgrave Macmillan.

19. It is quite common for leading figures from business or commerce to either chair the boards of cultural institutions or to serve on those boards.

20. Mijs, J.J.B. (2016). The unfulfillable promise of meritocracy: Three lessons and their implications for justice in education. *Social Justice Research* 29(1): p. 21.

21. Courtois, A. (2018). *Elite Schooling and Social Inequality: Privilege and Power in Ireland's Top Private Schools*. Basingstoke: Palgrave Macmillan.

22. See Courtois, A. op cit.

23. Ibid., p. 6.

24. Bourdieu, P. and Passeron, J.C. (1977). *Reproduction in Education, Society and Culture*. Beverly Hills: Sage; Courtois, A. (2018). *Elite Schooling and Social Inequality: Privilege and Power in Ireland's Top Private Schools*. Basingstoke: Palgrave Macmillan, p. 153.

25. These are groups that Bourdieu calls 'the disinherited'.

26. Williams, R. (1977). *Marxism and Literature*. Oxford: Oxford University Press.

27. Bourdieu, P. and Passeron, J.C. (1977). *Reproduction in Education, Society and Culture*. Beverly Hills: Sage; Courtois, A. (2018). *Elite Schooling and Social Inequality: Privilege and Power in Ireland's Top Private Schools*. Basingstoke: Palgrave Macmillan, p. 210.

28. Ibid., pp. 53–54.

29. Lynch, K. (2019). Inequality in education: What educators can and cannot change. In Connolly, M., Eddy-Spicer, D.H., James, C. and Kruse, S.D. (eds.). *The Sage Handbook of School Organization*. Los Angeles: Sage, pp. 301–317.

30. Piketty, T. (2014). *Capital in the Twenty-First Century*. Cambridge Mass.: Harvard University Press, p. 20.

31. Goldthorpe. J.H. (2007). *On Sociology: Volume Two – Illustrations and Retrospect*. 2nd ed. Stanford: Stanford University Press.

32. Piketty, T. (2014). *Capital in the Twenty-First Century*. Cambridge Mass.: Harvard University Press, p. 20.

33. Standing, G. (2011). *The Precariat: The New Dangerous Class*. London: Bloomsbury.

34. Marsh, J. (2011). *Class Dismissed: Why We Cannot Teach or Learn Our Way Out of Inequality*. New York: Monthly Review Press.

35. Streeck, W. (2016). *How Will Capitalism End?* London: Verso, p. 28.

36. Ibid., pp. 28–30.

37. Piketty, T. (2014). *Capital in the Twenty-First Century*. Cambridge Mass.: Harvard University Press, p. 22. Père Goriot is set in the early nineteenth century.

38. Ibid., p. 22.

39. hooks, b. (1984). *Feminist Theory: From Margin to Center*. Boston, MA: South End Press; hooks, b. (2010). *Teaching Critical Thinking: Practical Wisdom*. New York: Routledge.

40. Gloria Jean Watkins is bell hooks' birth name. hooks uses the lower case herself, hence its use here. When she published her first book in 1981, *Ain't I a Woman? Black Women and Feminism*, she chose the pseudonym 'bell hooks' in tribute to her mother and great-grandmother. She decided not to capitalise her new name to place focus on her work rather than her name, on her ideas rather than her personality.

41. Rancière, J. (1991). *The Ignorant Schoolmaster: Five Lessons in Intellectual Emancipation* (Ross, K., trans.). Stanford, CA: Stanford University Press.

42. Freire, P. (1970 [2000]). *Pedagogy of the Oppressed*. 30th anniversary edition with an introduction by Macedo, D. New York: Continuum.

43. Borg, C. and Mayo, P. (2007). *Public Intellectuals, Radical Democracy and Social Movements: A Book of Interviews*. New York: Praeger; Apple, M.W. (2013). *Can Education Change Society?* New York: Routledge.

44. We can see how effective it was in colonising Irish people as most Irish people now speak English and have done so for over 100 years.

45. Rancière, J. (1991). *The Ignorant Schoolmaster: Five Lessons in Intellectual Emancipation* (Ross, K., trans.). Stanford, CA: Stanford University Press.

46. Ibid., pp. 45–73.

47. Freire, P. (1970 [2000]). *Pedagogy of the Oppressed*. 30th anniversary edition with an introduction by Macedo, D. New York: Continuum.

48. Rancière, J. (1991). *The Ignorant Schoolmaster: Five Lessons in Intellectual Emancipation* (Ross, K., trans.). Stanford, CA: Stanford University Press, p. 102.

49. hooks, b. (1984). *Feminist Theory: From Margin to Center*. Boston, MA: South End Press; hooks, b. (2010). *Teaching Critical Thinking: Practical Wisdom*. New York: Routledge.

50.   Freire, P. (1970 [2000]). *Pedagogy of the Oppressed*. 30th anniversary edition with an introduction by Macedo, D. New York: Continuum, p. 72.

51.   Applied knowledge in the STEM subjects.

52.   Conaghan, D. (2015, October 3). Instrumental music education in Ireland: The canary in the coalmine of educational equality. Paper presented at the UCD School of Social Justice Annual Conference at UCD, Belfield.

53.   It cost about €1,000 upfront for a three-week summer camp in the Gaeltacht in 2019.

54.   Gardner, H. (1983). *Frames of Mind: The Theory of Multiple Intelligences*. New York: Paladin.

55.   Borg, C. and Mayo, P. (2007). *Public Intellectuals, Radical Democracy and Social Movements: A Book of Interviews*. New York: Praeger; Crean, M. and Lynch, K. (2011). Resistance, struggle and survival: The university as a site for transformative education. In O'Shea, A. and O'Brien, M. (eds), *Pedagogy, Oppression and Transformation in a 'Post-Critical' Climate*. London: Continuum International Publishing Group, pp. 51–68.

56.   Borg, C. and Mayo, P. (2007). *Public Intellectuals, Radical Democracy and Social Movements: A Book of Interviews*. New York: Praeger; Apple, M.W. (2015). Reframing the question of whether education can change society, *Educational Theory* 65(3): pp. 299–315; Ivancheva, M. (2017). Between permanent revolution and permanent liminality: Continuity and rupture in the Bolivarian government's higher education reform. *Latin American Perspectives* 44(1): pp. 251–266.

57.   Macedo, D. (2000). Introduction. In Freire, P. (ed.), Pedagogy of the Oppressed. New York: Bloomsbury Academic; Edling, S. and Mooney Simmie, G. (eds) (2020). *Democracy and Teacher Education: Dilemmas, Challenges and Possibilities*. UK: Routledge.

FREE THOUGHT, EDUCATION FOR SOCIAL CHANGE AND THE NEED FOR EDUCATIONAL REFORM

Garrett Phelan's *FREE THOUGHT FM* is fundamentally about equality and access to education. With this essay, I wish to explore some of the issues that for me are crucial to this topic in an Irish context. I will do this by outlining a way of thinking about education that I hope might broaden and deepen the debate around a question Garrett posed to me: 'what is education for?'

I will also argue that the single biggest impediment to real education, to equality and to structural change in the Irish education system – a system that not even a global pandemic can, it seems, budge – is the high-stakes terminal exam at second level that is the Leaving Certificate. I will look at: some of the issues created by our refusal to let go of this system; where this resistance to change comes from; and illustrate that, nevertheless, change is on the way and there are reasons to be cheerful.

• My own perspective and experience

When Garrett Phelan interviewed me as part of *FREE THOUGHT FM*,[1] he said in passing of my position as principal of a comprehensive school on the northside of Dublin that it was a 'very important role'. While I would in some ways agree, I was also at the time reminded of what Patrick Kavanagh wrote, that "[t]here is nothing as dead and as damned as an important thing".[2] So, informed by a variety of educational roles, all diversely important — as teacher, as youth worker, as teacher educator, as school principal, as policy networker and as educational researcher — but also remembering Kavanagh's caveat, I carry with me some perspectives which I should mention from the start:

- Yes, formal education and schooling are important, but they can be overrated. We need to be concerned about the quality and equality of education in schools, concerned with what schooling is all about, if we are to treat all the nation's children equally. From the perspective of equity and social change, it is important to recognise that non-formal, informal and lifelong learning are equally important, and in some respects even more important, to the formation and reformation of a nation.

- I have been honoured to be the Principal of Mount Temple Comprehensive School.[3] This is a school that has been, since its foundation, co-educational, inclusive, serving minorities, devoted to a broad global perspective, committed to justice and also devoted to excellence in learning in the arts. While my experience in Mount Temple proves to me that schools can act to critique, and even provide a laboratory for alternatives to, the dominant values in a society, I am also conscious that, for many, schools serve to maintain and reinforce inequity and injustice.[4]

- I have also been working at the interface of practice, policy and research in a field which in Europe for the past 20 years has been described as Global Education[5]

– an umbrella term for various types of education for social change, local and global, including development education, human rights education and education for sustainable development. This is education that opens people's eyes and minds to the realities of the world and enables them to take action for greater justice and sustainability.[6] So I have worked at the convergence of, on the one hand, education systems that may be understood to replicate the current status quo, and on the other, the work of education systems that open up possibilities for greater justice and sustainability. There is evidence that the latter are becoming more and more common in European countries.[7]

Finally, I am convinced that at the heart of the difference between education that maintains the status quo, and education that works towards a more just, more equal and more sustainable world, lie creativity, imagination and narrative – not a grand narrative, but small stories of significant change. For this reason, bringing artists and educators together in conversation is, I believe, crucial to the opening up of alternative possibilities, to what philosopher Richard Kearney described as 'the wake of imagination'.[8]

•   The purpose of education

To deepen the conversation, I want to return to the question that Garrett Phelan posed to me during our live broadcast conversation as part of *FREE THOUGHT FM:* 'what is education?' And I'd like to begin with a little thought experiment.

I want to bring you back to your own school days, back to a particular school, and a particular class full of 15-year-olds. Can you see it? Now, it is a wet Thursday afternoon in November. Can you smell it? Who is the teacher? Who are you sitting beside? What subject is being taught? What is the name of the school? Can you also recall the entrance hall? Did it have the school motto there? (Well, forget the school motto – what we are after is not what they *say* they *believe* in, but what those who lead the school believe education to be, as indicated by what is actually taught and learnt there.)

Like most schools, your remembered school had an operative model of education out of which it worked – a practical answer to the question that Garrett Phelan posed. This is often expressed in answer to the slightly different question, 'what is education for?' While there are myriad answers to that question, a history of human thought that goes back millennia, I would like to simplify a little. There are really four predominant models that can be used in the answering of this question. Let us imagine that they are represented in the four corners of the room you are now sitting in as you read this essay.

In the first corner, we have Model 1, which we might label the 'Academic Disciplines Model'. Within this model, the purpose of education is to pass on traditions of learning, to ensure that students excel in subject-based knowledge, to enable academic progress and development. If the school you are remembering operated from this model, we focus on deep subject knowledge, academic rigour and intellectual achievement. We might also focus on test results.

In the second corner of the room in which you now sit, we have Model 2, which we might label the 'Personal Development Model'. Within this predominant model, the purpose of education is to ensure personal development, individual growth, creativity and human flourishing. If our school operates out of this model, we want to ensure that those leaving the school are well-rounded human beings with the skills necessary to thrive as individuals.

In the third corner is Model 3, what we might call the 'Good Citizen Model'. Within this model, the purpose of education is to equip students to become decent citizens, understanding the way the world works, fitting in as useful members of society and making a contribution. (There is a narrower version of this model, beloved by some economists and economic think-tanks, which focuses on the importance of schooling for providing for 'labour market needs'.)

In the (far off) fourth corner, there is another, less prevalent model, which we might name the 'Social Justice Model' of education. According to this model, there is something deeply wrong with the world. Injustice abounds, inequality persists, our ecosystems are being destroyed, we are in trouble. Educators may have traditionally helped students to understand the world; the point with a Social Justice Model of education is to change it, towards greater justice, human rights for all and greater sustainability for people and planet. Rather than fitting into the world as it is, learners can imagine something better, and contribute to building it.

So, these are four models or ways of thinking about the question 'what is education?' They are, in some respects, 'ideal types' or slight caricatures. Not only is there no school on the planet that resides purely in any one model, but aspects of each model are required. If you need brain surgery, or advice on how to graft an apple tree, then here is hoping that the person performing the incision in each case has deep and practical knowledge of the subject (Model 1). We need students to leave school with some self-understanding as human beings, some ability to grow, develop, transcend boundaries, continue to learn, find joy in the world, form decent relationships and flourish as individuals (Model 2). Similarly, unless we take account of the needs of society, and the need for our students to understand and contribute to society, including the realities of the labour market (Model 3), we risk educating generations for disgruntlement and unemployment. So, there is no one model or type that is being either demoted or promoted here. Equally, it is important to recognise that not only do students need to understand and analyse and celebrate the world as it is, and to a certain extent fit into it comfortably, they also need to change it. The world needs changing; and students need the skills and developed talents necessary to discern the direction of that change in a future that only they can know and that we cannot (Model 4). Unless justice and sustainability form part of their repertoire, they may not have a liveable world to pass on to the next generation.

So, I'm suggesting that all four models are needed. Now, imagining that each of these four models is placed in a corner of the room you are currently in, bring to mind the school I asked you to remember earlier, and its operative model of education. We have just asserted that no school is an ideal type, so the school I asked you to remember on that wet Thursday afternoon is not in any one corner. Where on the floor between the differing models (in each of the corners) might you stand if you were to accurately represent where your remembered school resides, or resided, in terms of its operative model of education? Opposite is a little outline that might help.

If you wish, you can mark an X on the outline to help yourself visualise where your remembered school sits in this system.[9]

Now, depending on where in the world you went to school, and what sort of a school it was, you might stand, or mark the spot, somewhere between Model 1 and Model 2. In Ireland, I would suggest that, increasingly since the 1990s, schools have moved from somewhere between Models 1 and 2 to embrace or at least head in the direction of Model 3.

I would also like to suggest that if you have moved to corner 4, or your x marks a spot closer to 4, then you are in a tiny minority.

I have engaged in workshops that facilitate people in remembering, identifying and reflecting on the current education model in a variety of settings in Ireland, in Europe and beyond. I have probably run these workshops in different educational sectors over a hundred times, and with thousands of educators, educational leaders and policymakers, not only in schools, but also in youth, community, and adult and teacher education settings. In each case it is clear that while there may have been movement over the past three decades, from Model 1 to Model 2 to Model 3, and a combination thereof, in all settings, the neglected model turns out to be Model 4.

- **What does this mean for education, for equality and for the world?**

Each and every one of the three predominant models, while necessary, also contributes to ensuring that the world remains the way it is. These three models maintain the status quo, reinforce current inequities and systems of inequality and injustice, reinforce privilege and maintain poverty.

What the world needs now, what humanity requires, what nature and the earth are calling for, is a

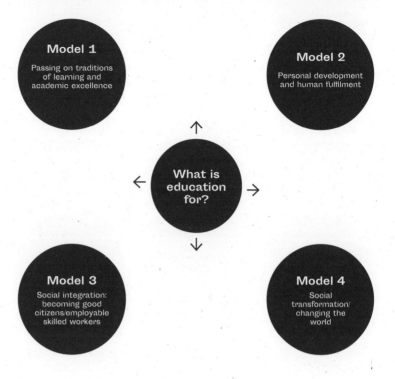

Models of Education

world of greater equality, greater justice, deeper solidarity, sounder ecological security and more sustainability. What is needed, from education and for education, is a move in the direction of that neglected fourth model. Unless, and until, education systems prioritise learning for greater justice over learning to maintain the current systems, and unless education is understood as a crucible for learning how to change the world towards greater justice and sustainability, then I believe that we are doomed.

But we are not doomed, as there are signs of hope. While this fourth model is, I believe, still the most neglected, the least prioritised of all four models, there are movements for change, throughout Europe and around the world, that are gathering experiences of integrating the fourth model into education systems, without neglecting the other three.[10]

- **The biggest obstacle to second-level education in Ireland: the Leaving Certificate**

There is a need for us to move from traditional educational models towards a social justice and social change model, without oversimplifying or neglecting the need for the existing models.

Nevertheless, whatever model of education a school might choose, there is one major impediment to educational improvement and reform that is particular to Ireland, not only regarding the need to move to more progressive models, but more fundamentally, regarding what should be the core purposes of an education system – student learning, care and well-being. The impediment that needs to be removed in the second-level education system in Ireland is the Leaving Certificate exam, and all the paraphernalia that surrounds it.[11]

The Leaving Certificate is the single biggest obstacle within the Irish education system to the improvement of that system: an impediment to teaching, to learning, to care, to well-being, to community, to student flourishing and to joy. While it impedes and prevents these core purposes of education, it also operates in such a way as to ensure that there is no possibility that education might contribute to greater societal equality. It is a national institution at the service of solidifying inequality.

The Leaving Certificate is a systemic evil. It needs to go. It does not need to be tinkered with or changed slightly or reformed — it needs to be totally demolished. Better to start from scratch than to start from where we are now.[12] As mentioned above, not even a global pandemic has affected our adherence to an institution that is outdated, divisive and damaging.

I have seen arguments emerge recently that suggest that students 'deserve' to have the full experience of the examination process. Anyone who has actually experienced being a victim of this system, having had to sit the exam, would not want to foist the experience on their children or students. It is an exam, not a study visit, not an immersion in learning – the only good thing about the experience is when it is over. (For many, it is so traumatic that they experience a forgetfulness, wanting to drive the experience from their mind; so, it resides in the nightmare realm).

I repeat myself: the Leaving Certificate exam is evil and it needs to go if we are ever to have a second-level school system that values education and learning over assessment and stratification, that values students over a notion of 'fairness' that is in truth deeply unfair and structurally unjust, and that values second-level education as a good in itself over selection for entry into third-level education.

I'd like to outline just some of the reasons why this high-stakes terminal exam doesn't work and needs to go.

Firstly, it is clear that the operation of the Leaving Certificate, prioritising as it does a particularly irrelevant and unnecessarily pressurised system of assessment, serves to reward certain types of 'learning' and regurgitation, and also rewards gaming the system rather than the acquisition of necessary skills, critical thinking or even broad and deep conceptual knowledge. In-depth research from colleagues in Trinity College and Dublin City University has shown, beyond any reasonable doubt, what those of us who have worked with the Leaving Certificate, or supported students in living through the experience, have known for a long time – that the Leaving Certificate encourages rote learning and neglects the skills and aptitudes that are actually necessary for living and thriving in the twenty-first century: creativity, intellectual rigour, inquisitiveness and critical thinking.[13] I would add that it also often murders love of learning and, with a few notable exceptions, promotes competition over collaboration.

Secondly, it is clear that the mode of assessment used in the Leaving Certificate negatively affects not only the nature and method of teaching in second-level schools, leading to 'teaching to the test', but also narrows and confines the content of the curriculum. This happens not only in the apotheosising of all that is measurable and testable, and confining to non-curriculum all that is not, but in a very real sense it also limits learning to those parts of the curriculum that are likely to 'come up'. This is not education, it is betting – the work, not of educators, but of bookmaker tipsters!

This putting the cart before the horse – assessment should be at the service of curriculum and learning, not vice versa – also has a 'backwash effect' on the rest of second-level education. This has ensured that, for example, thorough and effective reform of the Junior Cycle was impeded by the strange notion that teachers could not assess their own students (which every teacher already does), that there is something more worthy in an external 'examiner' (i.e. usually a teacher of other students) correcting blindly. It also has a more immediate effect, through the illogic that 'if students haven't any experience of high stakes exams at Junior Cycle level, how will they ever be able to sit the Leaving Certificate?'

Of course, in every school there are teachers who find ways around the system to ensure spaces for learning and freedom; and there is within certain subjects, and particularly within Transition Year, space for thorough and deep learning. But these spaces are tiny oases in the desert of learning that is large swathes of the Irish second-level education system. What causes this learning desertification? It's the Leaving Certificate, plain and simple.

Schools are primarily supposed to be about learning – but they are also, at their best, communities of care, an important aspect of school that has been amplified due to its loss during the pandemic. What distinguishes exceptional schools is the quality of this care, and the nature of caring relationships on which learning is based. While parents and families may be the primary educators, there are also situations in which schools can make all the difference in the world to a child in need of a little more care. The mark of a strong school community is not only how well learning takes place there, but how well students are cared for.

Unfortunately, at the heart of the Irish second-level school system there is a fundamental contradiction that undermines the core duty of care of schools. On the one hand, the State has put some considerable resources (if not enough!) into the promotion and provision of care and well-being in schools, with progressive and cumulative curricula, etc.

But this is completely undermined by the Leaving Certificate, which is, I say not only from the empirical evidence but from direct experience, the single most significant cause of unnecessary anxiety and the most detrimental factor in student mental health and well-being in the final years of second-level education. It is as though the State were saying, 'let's build them up with well-being programmes in the early years, then pull the rug from under them by insisting on an unnecessary high-stakes exam at the end'.

And to add insult to injury, the State then provides 'special accommodation' in the exams for those suffering anxieties caused by, yes you've guessed it, the Leaving Certificate exam system.

So, in terms of learning, the Leaving Certificate is defunct and counterproductive. In terms of student care and well-being, it is unnecessary and downright evil.

'But what about determining entry into third level?' This is a frequent question posed in response to calls to dismantle the Leaving Certificate. There are better ways. Unfortunately, the Leaving Certificate is not that effective as a selection process for third level, and there are a growing number of university leaders in Ireland who are speaking clearly about this.

Fortunately, there are plenty of alternatives and very different models of third-level entry selection processes available. But I would also suggest that, for the learning and well-being of second-level students, second-level education should be determined not by the selection (and social stratification) needs of third-level institutions, but by the learning and care needs of second-level students. The current system is not only a case of the tail wagging the dog, but another tail entirely from the neighbour's bigger dog wagging our little dog!

- **Reform is necessary, but there will be resistance to reform**

So, in case I have not yet repeated the proposition often enough – the Leaving Certificate is evil and must go. Thankfully, there is a possibility of reform on the way. This can be seen in the growing calls for change from university provosts, leading educators and educational researchers, student representatives, parent bodies, school management and principal networks, economists, leading analysts of labour market needs, industry leaders, human rights advocates and even education journalists. There is a strong and growing voice in favour of reform. There is also a process already underway (more of which below).

Nevertheless, it should also be clearly stated that there are vested interests at stake, individuals who are vocally and vehemently opposed to Leaving Certificate reform, as they were to Junior Cycle reform. These individuals and institutions are invested in keeping things the way they are, maintaining the status quo. They are interested parties that I assume will pile on and target those willing to call out the need for radical reform. Advocates and apologists of the Leaving Certificate – be they politicians, grind school owners, trade union industrial relations negotiators, newspaper sellers, TV advertising executives, certain guidance counsellors making a few bob on the side by teaching students how to game the system and get the most marks, contrarians and sadists ('I went through it and it did me no harm') – all have vested interests in keeping things the way they are.

I mention these players in the drama that may unfold in regard to reform as I think it is necessary to recognise that there will be resistance to change and there will be campaigns to maintain the status quo. Unfortunately, while some of those resisting reform have direct vested interests (e.g. grind schools), and some more indirect (media outlets that profit from the melee and hype, while students suffer), there are some who are not just misguided, but see direct leverage for (in some cases very valid) industrial relations claims, by impeding reform. The claims may be valid, but the use of resistance to reform as a leverage in industrial action is not. This is, to my mind, sad – because we know that we cannot implement effective reform without strong teacher involvement. But unfortunately, in the recent past regarding Junior Cycle reform, some teaching unions were arguing against trusting teachers. This is not a principled stance, but a negotiating tactic.

I trust teachers, for the most part. The best teachers, the vast majority of teachers, want what's best for their students, and want quality learning and real care. Reform of the Leaving Certificate could be liberating for teachers. This is important and many teachers I know support reform. But the even more important point is that schools should be liberating, and caring, and promoting learning for students. They will not be, and cannot be, until the Leaving Certificate is radically reformed.

However, it is not only those who are resistant to change that will impede real root and branch Senior Cycle reform. We do not have a culture of reform in Ireland. While acknowledging real progressive change in some regards in recent years, such as the development of the Leaving Certificate Applied and some new subject courses, the overall turgidity and stasis in the system is remarkable.

But this is not that surprising when viewed from a comparative or cultural perspective. In many countries there is a culture of regular reform – the world changes, we learn more and more about how and why and when people learn, and so curriculum, and the assessment methods that should be subservient to curriculum, should also change – not for the sake of change, but because that is what student learning needs and what the world requires. The Irish education system has not had a culture of root and branch reform and introducing a culture of change will take time. This will, I hope, begin to shift, not for change's sake, but for the sake of students' learning and care.

Reasons to be cheerful: in Ireland, in Europe and globally

There is change on the way, and while there will be resistance, change is necessary; reform of the Leaving Certificate is gathering momentum and will prevail. Very recent announcements from the NCCA, the Department of Education, the Department of Higher Education and other stakeholders – particularly student representatives – really do hold promise for real and necessary change.

One real ray of hope in this process is the model of reflection on reform that the NCCA (National Council for Curriculum and Assessment), with the assistance of the ESRI (Economic and Social Research Institute), has led in recent years. This process was broadly consultative and representative in nature. Informed by the best international research and by comparative analysis of different school systems, the process gathered, at grassroots school level, the views of all stakeholders – students, parents, teachers, school management. It is clear from this process that there is an appetite for reform, and a need for reform.

As I write we are living through a pandemic, and so I really do not want to sound like I am operating under a naivety or false optimism. There are many signs of resistance to change in the system, and the fact that, while huge and apparently unmovable swathes of Irish institutions changed radically during the pandemic, the thing that seemed most impermeable to change was the dogged reluctance to abandon the high-stakes assessment model – well, it does not augur well. In this context, it may sound naïve to argue that change is just around the corner.

Nevertheless, there are other clear signs, both in other European countries and more globally, that high-stakes terminal tests are being rejected as detrimental to learning. This movement brings hope.

More broadly, this recent pandemic has led to a deeper conversation about the nature and future of schooling, and also to a reassessment of values relating to education, including values of solidarity. There is also a growing recognition of the importance of global interdependence. Without wishing to in any way diminish the huge difficulties we have encountered, I believe that there are reasons to be cheerful, not only regarding impending Leaving Certificate reform, but also in regard to the slow but inexorable movement of education towards greater justice, greater solidarity and greater sustainability. In a very real sense, the future is unwritten.

Endnotes

1. Garrett Phelan, in conversation with Liam Wegimont as part of *FREE THOUGHT FM*. Available at: https://freethoughtfm.bandcamp.com/track/day-2-liam-wegimont-mount-temple-comprehensive-school.

2. "What seems of public importance is never of any importance … There is nothing as dead and damned as an important thing. The things that really matter are casual, insignificant little things, things you would be ashamed to talk of publicly." Kavanagh, P. (1964). *Self-Portrait*. Dublin: Dolmen Press, p. 20–21.

3. Mount Temple Comprehensive is a co-educational school on the northside of Dublin which has for almost 50 years had an ethos of inclusion and celebrating diversity. Its motto is 'All Different, All Equal', and its mission statement asserts that it is a school "increasingly devoted to education for sustainable development and global justice". More information available at: https://mounttemple.ie/.

4. See Kathleen Lynch's essay in this book.

5. GENE works towards the day when all people in Europe – in solidarity with peoples globally – will have access to quality Global Education. The views expressed in this article are that of the author, and do not represent the views of GENE, its Ministries or Agencies, nor the European Commission. More information available at: https://gene.eu/.

6. For more on this Maastricht definition of Global Education and other related areas see: Nygaard, A. and Wegimont, L. (2018). Global Education in Europe: Concepts, Definitions and Aims. Dublin: GENE.

7. See, for example Bourn, D. (ed.). (2020). *The Bloomsbury Handbook on Global Education and Learning*. London: Bloomsbury.

8. Kearney, R. (1988). *The Wake of Imagination*. London: Hutchinson.

9. But please don't ruin the book, which I presume is a thing of beauty!!! :).

10. For more on this, with examples from a variety of European countries, see McAuley, J. (2020). The State of Global Education in Europe. Dublin: GENE. Available at: https://gene.eu/.

11. I should re-iterate that I write this in a personal capacity, not as the Principal of Mount Temple Comprehensive nor as the Executive Director of GENE (www.gene.eu). Nevertheless, my position is informed by my experience as a school principal in Ireland over 15 years, where conversations with brilliant students, engaged parents, inspiring teachers, visionary Board members and some progressive colleague school principals inform my position, as does experience through GENE over 20 years with colleagues from, for example, the Finnish National Board of Education/EDUFIN. On this latter, see for example Jaaskelainen, L., Wegimont, L., *et al.* (eds). (2012). Becoming a Global Citizen: Proceedings of the International Conference on Competencies of Global Citizens. FNBE/GENE: Helsinki/Dublin. I am particularly indebted to Dr Jeremy Jones, former chair, and Professor Anne Lodge, current chair, of the Board of Mount Temple, and to Helen Gormley, current Acting Principal, for many conversations regarding whether the Leaving Certificate is a necessary evil, or just evil.

12. Anyone who says 'we can't change it until we have a better alternative' is a) invested in maintaining an unjust structure and b) knows little about the process of curriculum reform. The same argument was used for the maintenance of the slave trade, if I'm not mistaken.

13. Brown, M., Burns, D., Devitt, A., McNamara, G. and O'Hara, J. (2018). Is it all memory recall? An empirical investigation of intellectual skills requirements in Leaving Certificate examination papers in Ireland. *Irish Educational Studies* 37(3). London: Taylor & Francis.

SORTING
THE CITY

For many Dubliners, the river Liffey forms a significant division, between quality to the south and poverty to the north. For many years, and until early in 2019, a billboard advertising a popular drink on the bridge that took trains across Lower Gardiner Street asked Dubliners passing beneath whether they were a 'North Cider or South Cider?' In 2015, convalescent beds at Mount Carmel community hospital in south Dublin were empty because "of a reluctance of northside patients to cross the Liffey".[1] In fact, the hospital was five kilometres south of the city and at some distance from public transportation, little bother to car-owning folk but an expensive hurdle for others. Provision in the south and hardship in the north; these differences are the result of the way the territory of the city is marked out and managed. There is nothing casual about the social geography of Dublin. It has always been inherently political.

The allocation of responsibilities (for example, for housing or education) and of differing tax-raising capacities to different levels of government (national, regional, local) sets the framework for local government and planning. It also places limits on the extent of revenue-sharing and resource-pooling across local areas. The size and autonomy of these local units is likewise significant. One of the attractions of suburbs has been that the problems of the city are left behind and, with political autonomy, the cost of those problems can also be avoided.

For these reasons, it can seem important to keep the suburbs apart from the city and this is what has been done at various times by the people of the suburbs to the south of Dublin as they have resisted incorporation into the city. Beyond this, they have also been able in the same manner to prevent the march of public housing into their neighbourhoods, directing, by default, the rehousing of the working class from the inner-city slums towards the north and the west.

Sorting the city in this way, the residents of south Dublin note their own distinction and above-average house prices and land values, and insist that certain sorts of neighbours would be toxic to this distinction. Therefore, they campaign against such facilities as housing for Traveller families. Finally, they seek to pass this distinction and advantage to their children through a fragmented education system that allows postcode to determine school entry. With schools serving generally wealthy families, the parents of south Dublin can top up the quality of local education and thereby queue-jump their children into the best third-level courses and colleges.

- ## The city and the suburbs

By the mid-nineteenth century, Dublin had more or less grown into the space between the canals, the Royal to the north and the Grand to the south (see map on following page). From the 1840s, new railways anchored a necklace of suburbs, particularly along the coastline running south

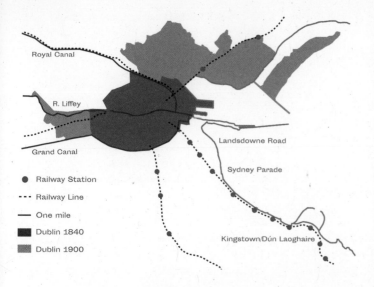

Royal Canal

R. Liffey

Grand Canal

● Railway Station
--- Railway Line
— One mile
■ Dublin 1840
▨ Dublin 1900

Landsdowne Road

Sydney Parade

Kingstown/Dún Laoghaire

The Extension of the City
of Dublin by the Dublin
Corporation Act 1900

of the city towards Kingstown (present day Dún Laoghaire). Some, who could afford it, now chose to work in the city but live further out. Each evening, they left a city increasingly notorious for some of the worst slum housing in Europe.[2] As they crossed the Grand Canal they also escaped the fiscal grip of the Corporation of the City of Dublin. The people who journeyed home from Westland Row to Landsdowne Road, Sandymount or Sydney Parade slept in the township of Pembroke to which they paid rates, and similarly for the next few stations, hosted by Blackrock township, and then on to Kingstown township. Likewise, the commuters who left Harcourt Street stepped out of the city into the township of Rathmines and Rathgar once they too had crossed the Grand Canal. This injured the Corporation and in 1899 it petitioned the government of the United Kingdom for the opportunity to annex Pembroke, Blackrock, Kingstown, Rathmines and Rathgar to its south, New Kilmainham to its west, and Clontarf, Drumcondra and Glasnevin to its north.

Speaking to a Select Committee of the House of Lords, counsel for the Corporation said that Dublin "had been made poor by the great exodus of the rich and wealthy classes into the suburbs".[3] Further, the separation of classes allowed the suburbs to charge themselves a local tax at a rate about half of that in the city. Unwilling to share expenses, the ratepayers of the outlying townships petitioned against their annexation. To a Select Committee on Local Government in Ireland, a commissioner for the Pembroke township proposed that the "increase of taxation which would be consequent upon annexation would stop building in the township", while a property owner in Rathmines claimed that it would "send the people off to districts beyond, and [would] ruin the townships".[4] In the event, the Dublin Corporation Act of 1900 annexed the districts to the north and west but did not interfere with those to the south (see map above).[5] Some later annexations, as in 1930, were more even-handed but on each occasion where there was a geographical imbalance in the expansion of the city, the trajectories of least resistance were towards the north and west, while the barricades against incorporation always proved most effective in the south.

The comparative ease with which the city could stretch north and west has meant that this was where it found lands when it was disposed to build social housing.

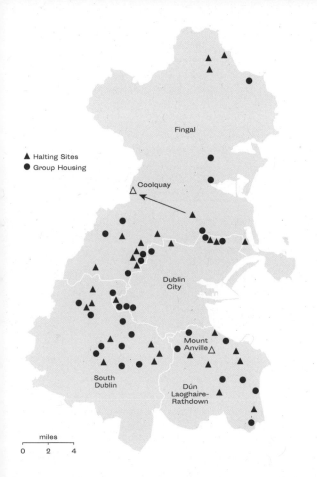

▲ Halting Sites
● Group Housing

Fingal

Coolquay

Dublin
City

Mount
Anville

South
Dublin

Dún
Laoghaire-
Rathdown

miles

0   2   4

Official Traveller
Accommodation, 2018

Thus, south Dublin has neighbourhoods of private housing, and social housing estates have largely been kept out of these districts.

● **Nimbyism and the right to the city**

In the 1930s and 1940s, the Corporation of the City of Dublin built over 17,000 homes, some of them in small-scale, four-storey developments near the centre of the city, on land it owned.[6] This allowed for workers to live near their employment, as well as to take easy advantage of the shopping, leisure and recreation possibilities of the city centre. Whereas middle-class people could afford to travel to whatever amenities they desired, these developments gave the least advantaged an equal and effective right to the city.[7] This right is often contested.

For a BBC radio documentary called *The Travelling People*, Ewan MacColl wrote the 'The Moving On Song' (1960), about people who are unwelcome as neighbours. Its chorus is the essence of nimbyism: 'You'd better get born in some place | Move along, get along, move along, get along | Go, move, shift'. In 1975, musician Christy Moore added new verses and in bringing it home to Dublin highlighted the hostility towards Travellers: 'Mary Joyce was living at the side of the road | No halting place and no fixed abode | The vigilantes came to the Darndale site | And they shot her son in the middle of the night'. As conceded by Dublin City Council: "Local opposition to Traveller Accommodation can be significant."[8] In fact, the only sites provided specifically for Travellers to live together are at the very edges of the city (see map above). There can be few more striking images of marginality than this map of official provision for Travellers.[9] When it was proposed in 2018 to close one halting site, Collinstown, so that Dublin Airport might get a new runway, Fingal County Council took the opportunity to propose relocation to the very edge of Fingal, at Coolquay (see same map). One hundred people lived at Coolquay yet Fingal County Council received 600 'observations' objecting to the relocation.[10] The new housing, it was urged, would curtail the flood-plain on which the people of Coolquay depended for their own protection from inundation during storms.

Seeking election to the council of Dún Laoghaire-Rathdown in 2014, Josepha Madigan of Fine Gael averred that it would be a "dreadful waste of taxpayers' money" to allocate as a halting site expensive land in wealthy south Dublin.[11] The former council depot at Mount Anville (see previous map) had been proposed as a place for Traveller housing in 1989 and this use was outlined as part of official local authority plans in 2009. Nevertheless, in 2019 the Traveller housing was dropped from the plan.[12] It is as if poor people have no business living on valuable land. The rich ask that the poor live anywhere at all, but 'Not In My Back Yard'.

Time after time, working-class people have been told to go, move, shift. During boom times, developers eye greedily the inner-city sites on which poorer people live. Quite often the existing housing is in poor repair. We see this in Dublin today, with some of the council flats built in the 1930s coming under fire. Although of historical significance, Dublin City Council has started the process to delist both Pearse House and Markievicz House, which lie just south of the river at the heart of the city centre.[13]

This process would allow for their demolition. Of course, residents have been reassured that they will be rehoused in the vicinity but they would be wise to be sceptical. In inner-city north Dublin, social housing from the 1960s was demolished in 2012 but the former residents still await the new social housing units that were promised for the site on Lower Dominick Street. Even when public housing is cleared from a site and rebuilding goes ahead, government policy now dictates that this land be given over primarily for private development with council tenancies to comprise no more than 10% of the units built.[14] Where local authorities demand more than this request, an appeal by the developer to the Minister for Housing should readily secure a more modest request. Dublin City Council are finding this to be exactly the case with the redevelopment of the northside's O'Devaney Gardens, a site that formerly had universal public housing and now has no more than an indication from the developer that it might entertain requests for 30% social housing. Simon Coveney blocked a proposal for the development of the site as 100% social housing in 2016, when he was Minister for Housing, Planning, Community and Local Government.[15] Given that the law only requires 10% social housing, it will be interesting to see if the 30% commitment is realised. Commercial developers are effectively disqualifying a working-class right to the city. In the neighbourhood near Pearse House, Hibernia Real Estate Investment Trust has renovated a commercial property as One Cumberland Place. Behind this is St Andrew's Court, a block of social housing, and the CEO of Hibernia REIT has asked Dublin City Council that this be demolished as it is a "serious eyesore" which is "dragging down the quality of the street".[16]

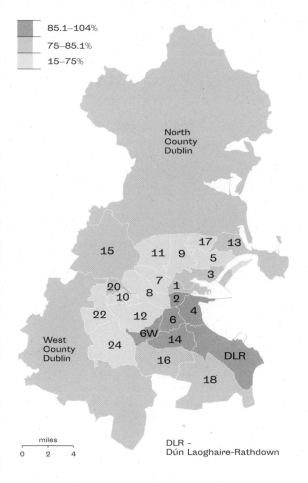

North
County
Dublin

15 11 9 17 13
5
3
20 7 1
10 8 2
22 12 4
6
6W 14
West
County 24 16 DLR
Dublin
18

miles
0 2 4

DLR -
Dún Laoghaire-Rathdown

Progression to College (%)
by Dublin Postcodes

Education and the reproduction of privilege

One of the ways that privilege is passed from one generation to the next is through education. Money can buy books, room for quiet study at home, supplementary grinds and a favourable postcode. As long as schools may recruit by postcode, they will reinforce class-based segregation. This is striking in Dublin.

There is a cone of privilege extending southwards from the city centre. If we map (see left) the proportion of people going from school to college, the districts with the schools most likely to send students to college form a coherent band on the southside (Dublin postal districts 2, 4, 6, 6W and 14, and the part of Dún Laoghaire-Rathdown outside the numbered Dublin postcodes).[17] In 2019, 3,360 students in this area sat the Leaving Certificate; of these students, 95% went on to third-level education. The ten districts with the lowest ratio of progression beyond school likewise form a coherent group, a crescent shape to the north and west from Darndale to Tallaght (Dublin postal districts 5, 7, 8, 9, 10, 11, 12, 17, 22 and 24). In 2019, 2,162 or 57% of those who took the Leaving Certificate at schools in this area went on to third-level education. In part, this contrast reflects the advantage that wealthier parents buy for their children when they send them to a fee-paying school. In those six southside districts, half the students sitting the Leaving Certificate did so in a fee-paying school. There is not a single fee-paying school in any of the ten low-progression districts flanking the city to its north and west. This is not the full story because, while the progression ratio for fee-paying schools in the privileged southside wedge is 107%, it was 83% for the 22 state-funded schools in the same area, way beyond the 57% for the 62 state schools in the group of less successful districts.[18]

By residence, and then by paying fees, parents confer significant privilege on their children. Being more likely to get to college, their children can expect a healthy graduate premium. In Ireland, people with an honours degree can expect double the salary of those with nothing beyond the Leaving Certificate.[19] School fees are a top-up to get better-than-average treatment. The people that can afford this are largely in the south of the city and that is why their fee-paying schools are there, and not in the crescent of disadvantage to the north and west. Even without paying fees, geography gifts advantage. By living in the catchment area of the more successful state schools, parents give their children a leg-up. Parents are buying this premium on the cheap. The salaries of teachers in all these schools, both non-fee-paying and fee-paying, both highly successful and less successful, are paid by the state.

The sorted city

The privilege defended by the southern suburbs resisting incorporation in the late-nineteenth century was replicated in the geography of social housing provision from the 1930s onwards, and is now protected by state-funded education and the ability of local communities to keep unwelcome neighbours away through pressure put on the planning system. For the United States, Bill Bishop warns of the dangers of the sorted city.[20] If people live in communities that are relatively homogeneous, they are less likely to support policies that use general funds to benefit groups other than themselves. In fact, they seem more likely to consider others a threat to their well-being and way of life. From Northern Ireland, we know that the minority of schools that are integrated by religion induce greater tolerance of other religions among their pupils.[21] From the United States, we know that children in schools largely segregated by race have fewer friends of another race and more negative attitudes towards other races.[22] From the United Kingdom, we know that, even controlling for class, children in class-segregated private schools believe that the pay of members of the elite should be higher than do children from state schools, and they are also less likely to agree that there is any social injustice in current levels of social inequality.[23] The sorted city undermines social solidarity. Perhaps we need a different sort of Dublin.

1. Cullen, P. (2015, September 5). Northside patients won't cross Liffey for empty hospital beds. *The Irish Times*.

2. Prunty, J. (1998). *Dublin Slums 1800–1925: A Study In Urban Geography*. Dublin: Irish Academic Press.

3. Dublin Boundaries Bill. (1899, July 25). *Times* [London], p. 5.

4. British Parliamentary Papers. (1880). c. 2725, xxx, 327. *Royal Com. to inquire into Boundaries and Municipal Areas of Cities and Towns in Ireland. Report, Part I., Evidence, Appendix (Dublin, Rathmines, etc.)*, qq. 4948, 4472.

5. Dublin Corporation Act 1900 (63 & 64 Vict. c.cclxiv).

6. Kelly, O. (2019, February 8). A century of housing: How the state built Ireland's homes. *The Irish Times*.

7. Lefebvre, H. (1996). The right to the city [1968], trans. Eleonore Kofman and Elizabeth Lebas. In Lefebvre, H. *Writings on Cities*. Oxford: Blackwell, pp. 108–123.

8. Dublin City Council. (2018). *Traveller Accommodation Programme* 2019–24. Dublin: Dublin City Council; Crowley, Ú. (2009). Outside in Dublin: Travellers, society and the state, 1963–1985. Canadian Journal of Irish Studies 35(1), pp. 17–24.

9. Dublin City Council, *Traveller Accommodation*; Dún Laoghaire-Rathdown County Council. (2018). *Traveller Accommodation Programme 2019–2024*. Dún Laoghaire: Dún Laoghaire-Rathdown County Council; Fingal County Council. (2018). *Traveller Accommodation Programme 2019–2024*. Swords: Fingal County Council; South Dublin County Council. (2018). *Traveller Accommodation Programme 2019–2024*. Tallaght: South Dublin County Council.

10. Holland, K. (2018, July 9). Traveller halting site gets approval from Fingal councillors. *The Irish Times*.

11. Holland, K. (2014, April 11). FG candidates accused of playing 'Traveller card'. *The Irish Times*.

12. Kelly, O. (2019, March 29). South Dublin council drops plans for Traveller housing in Mount Merrion. *The Irish Times*.

13. Kelly, O. (2018, November 12). Dublin city centre flats complexes to be demolished to allow for 'decent modern accommodation'. *The Irish Times*.

14. So-called Section V housing introduced in the Planning and Development Act 2000, and modified by Urban Regeneration and Housing Act 2015.

15. Kapila, L. (2019, November 6). Councillors vote through deal to redevelop O'Devaney Gardens after fraught debate. *Dublin Inquirer*.

16. Kapila, L. (2019, May 22). Developer in South Docklands urged council to demolish rundown social housing. *Dublin Inquirer*.

17. Feeder School Tables 2019. (2019, December 3). *The Irish Times*. Available at: https://irishtimes.com/polopoly_fs/1.4102952.1575355825!/menu/standard/file/feeders2019.pdf.

18. Some institutions of higher education report all the schools attended by their entrants and with some children moving schools this can produce an over-count of pupils, hence a figure like 107% as reported here. McGuire, P. (2019, December 3). Feeder school list: How to read it. *The Irish Times*.

19. Expert Group on Future Funding for Higher Education. (2015). *The Role, Value and Scale of Higher Education in Ireland. Dublin: Department of Education and Skills*. Available at: https://education.ie/en/The-Education-System/Higher-Education/Higher-Education-Role-Value-and-Scale-of-Higher-Education-in-Ireland-Discussion-Paper-1-.pdf, p. 19.

20. Bishop, B. (2008). *The Big Sort: Why the Clustering of Like-minded America is Tearing Us Apart*. Boston: Houghton Mifflin.

21. Stringer, M., Irwing, P., Giles, M., McClenahan, C., Wilson, R. and Hunter, J.A. (2009). Intergroup contact, friendship quality and political attitudes in integrated and segregated schools in Northern Ireland. *British Journal of Educational Psychology 79*, pp. 239–257.

22.   Joyner, K. and Kao, G. (2000). School racial composition and adolescent racial homophily. *Social Science Quarterly 81*(3), pp. 810–825.

23.   Evans, G. and Tilley, J. (2012). Public divisions: The influence of fee-paying education on social attitudes. In Park, A., Clery, E., Curtice, J., Phillips, M., and Utting, D. (eds.), *British Social Attitudes 28*. London: Sage, pp. 37–52.

BACK TO THE FLATS: HOUSING AND CLASS — ARCHITECTURES, NOVELS AND LODGERS

Part I: Implicit class – in the novel

In the recent Booker Prize-winning novel by Bernardine Evaristo, *Girl, Woman, Other*, Nigerian migrant Bummi laments the anglicisation of her daughter Carole. While ostensibly an account of a disenfranchised migrant widow, watching her daughter move away from Nigerian culture – the breakfast of yam porridge rejected for a cup of sugarless coffee – the story is most compelling in how it highlights the class implications of education. Bummi watches, always in judgement, as her daughter moves from local comprehensive to 'rich university' to an investment bank in London city. She watches as Carole begins to look "haughtily around their cosy little flat as if it was now a fleapit" having spent time at a university friend's family manor, with "more rooms than a housing estate."[1]

Eventually, "Bummi watched Carole as she stepped into the urine-smelling lift

to take her down to the ground level.

Her daughter would soon belong to them."[2]

By situating the drama in and around the micro-space of Bummi's high-rise London flat, Evaristo emphasises the role of the home in this story of social mobility, and racial frustration and fluidity. Domestic habits become socio-political allegories: the patterns of rice buying, daily yam porridge, the photocopied degree from the 'rich university' placed around the flat, even stuck on the back of the bathroom door. The small flat has, of course, an orbit representing Bummi's public world. And of course, this orbit circles the flat, but always, the flat and its disclosure of the intimate remains at the story's centre, reflecting both the everyday relevance and extraordinary implications of home.

Evaristo's portrait is just one of thousands from literature, television or art history that might be used to introduce the compelling nature of home in our lives: home as backdrop, as Third Man protagonist or as activating force. We have, since Freudian times at least, argued that how we live is who we are, home being the domain of our psychological selves. In these many readings, by thinkers like Gaston Bachelard, Martin Heidegger, Rom Carré and more recently, Anthony Vidler, home captures how we are spatially constructed. Almost as a conflation of 'being' and 'dwelling', home is the very site of self-realisation.

Much of these psychological and sensory reckonings around home's essential nature come from the premise of common experience; that is, we all share the common experience of a dusty corner or a kitchen odour or a sharp light from a bedroom window (Figures 1–2). In Evaristo's novel, that common experience of the domestic is usefully undone. The social reality of home is laid bare by the urine stench in the lift to the high-rise flat. If anything, there is no common experience of home in this episode: the fraught relationship between Nigerian mother and British daughter gapes as a social chasm, a breach defined by 'flea-pit flat' versus 'family

Figure 1, Domestic Moments.
Photograph by.author, 2020

Figure 2, Domestic Moments.
Photograph by author, 2020

Figure 3, Edenmore Housing Estate, Dublin
Corporation, 1963. Source: G. + T. Crampton
Photographic Archive, UCD Digital Library

manor'. In the book, Evaristo rightly sketches a racially, sexually and socially-stratified portrait of contemporary Britain through housing types; we move from urban to rural to suburban, from flat to commune to semi-D to farm settlement. Layers of difference seep out, dripping through housing descriptions and, in the end, capturing the visceral reality of living in twenty-first-century Britain.

In thinking more locally on housing types I am reminded of the uncanny relevance of Roddy Doyle's Barrytown trilogy for pre-Celtic Tiger Dublin; of how Doyle's dialogue-driven prose unpacked the trials and tribulations of working-class communities tossed to the edges of Dublin in new-ish 1970s housing estates. Or of the grit and spice of Cork city and its suburban enclaves as voiced in Lisa McInerney's *Glorious Heresies* (2015), where McInerney's hero Ryan comes from a single-parent criminal family in a council house and whose life-chances are ultimately pitched against those of his sweetheart, Karine. Karine comes from a slightly 'better' council estate and consequently makes 'better' choices (passes her exams, becomes a nurse, pays her taxes). Again, as in the example of Bummi and her daughter, the common experiences and universalism of home are jettisoned in favour of a socially stratified, conflicted and specified home, layered in long held and deeply nuanced ideas of class and difference.

• Part II: Class imperatives — houses or flats?

From flat to manor, council house to suburban housing estate, housing class itself underpins these various novelistic portrayals. In the end, it all comes back to where their characters are brought up, how they 'came up'; like a psycho-geography of origins, forming social-neural networks and determining tastes and tendencies thereafter. Defined only in the late 1960s as a category of academic (sociological) consideration,[3] the concept of 'housing class' assumes that there is some kind of unitary value system to which everyone aspires: that is, the single-family suburban house ideal. And from an Irish perspective, this is certainly the case. In fact, the suburban house model has driven Irish architectural history over the past century. I would go so far as to assert that Irish social history could be most comprehensively summed up by the suburban house and its social mores; that the waxing and waning of the construction of this type of house tells us more about Ireland's economic and cultural prerogatives, at least since the 1920s, than any political archive could (Figure 3). With booms of such house building occurring every second decade, from the 1930s through the 1990s, both public and private housing development in Ireland was dominated by the two-storey terraced or semi-detached individual home. Set onto abstract patterned roadways with pockets of front and back gardens, these pitched-roof, pebble-dash or brick-clad concrete boxes became the image of twentieth-century Ireland.

The monopoly of this house type arose out of economics and social aspirations, i.e. housing class. From the outset, and the dawn of the 1931/2 housing legislation, once-green fields were concreted and overlaid with water, waste and lighting services; terraces and crescents of repetitive houses could be built with speed and at reasonable cost. In Dublin at least, this construction pattern on virgin sites at the city's rural edge worked in stark contrast to housing development in the city centre where urban development took the form of four-storey flat blocks, on slum and brownfield sites. However, as a result of the higher costs involved in building in historic centres — compensations, complicated foundations and more — flat blocks were soon found to be too expensive and their residents were charged lower rents. This last point is crucial and in part establishes how, within the history of Irish housing typologies over the past nine decades, there emerged a specific psycho-social hierarchy which led to a preference, both socially and spatially, for the individual suburban family home.

Furthermore, according to a tribunal from 1938 (published in 1943 as the *Enquiry into the Housing of the Working Classes*),[4] flats were not only twice as expensive to construct but they had already, in less than a decade, become associated with the poorest of the poor. As a soft-modernist alternative to the new suburban house and taking their design cues from 1910s Holland and mid-war Britain, over 1,000 city-centre flats were built in Dublin during the 1930s and 1940s. They were allocated to the most casual of workers and those least able to afford the rent in the new far-flung housing estates. Offering snug, self-contained homes with indoor toilets and sculleries, the flats certainly represented domestic improvement to tenement dwellers. The mostly redbrick expressionist scheme blocks made new street fronts and, rising to four storeys, were reminiscent of Dublin's Georgian vernacular with its brick and window pattern (Figure 4). Accessed by

Figure 4, Brick (public) elevations,
St Joseph's Mansions/Aldborough
Court, Dublin Corporation, 1937-42.
Source: G. + T. Crampton Photographic
Archive, UCD Digital Library

Figure 5, Deck access (private) elevations,
St Joseph's Mansions/Aldborough
Court, Dublin Corporation, 1937-42.
Source: G. + T. Crampton Photographic
Archive, UCD Digital Library

communal decks, each flat had its own front door and coal chute. And their inhabitants' private lives were disclosed to the rear of each block, with large courts sporting pram sheds, drying sheds, bicycle sheds and meagre playgrounds (Figure 5). Yet, despite their ready acceptance into former slum communities, these flats were deemed cramped and unhealthy by many housing professionals at the time. In 1952, an Irish Times editorial described how:

[f]or thirty years or more this newspaper has raised its voice against the building of tenement flats to rehouse the dispossessed slum-dwellers of Dublin City. [...] so strong are the arguments against central blocks of flats [...] they are very considerably dearer than houses of similar capacity on virgin sites [...] they waste space which might suitably be devoted to the City's enrichment. [Flats] are dangerous to young life. However well equipped with playgrounds a modern block of flats may be, the children will not be restrained from running into the roadways [...] they cannot be as healthy as houses in the pure air of remoter suburbs [...] they are not 'homes'. They cannot satisfy that instinct which exists in nearly every Irish man and woman to possess a 'home of their own', when the same landing is shared with half a dozen other families.[5]

What is not considered by this middle-class editorial is how these flats, already by 1952, were homes to thousands of Dubliners. Furthermore, when Dublin Corporation allocations worked smoothly, extended families and generations of families occupied blocks, forming resilient communities, which, along with their acceptable architecture, have led to the quiet and dogged persistence of flats in the city. So, why then their consistent undervaluing in terms of housing provision? The answer is one of class, rooted in history and Irish social mores.

Flat blocks appeared as one of three things through their forty-year period of development in Dublin, from the 1930s to the 1970s: firstly, as a slum-clearance solution; or secondly, as a necessary evil; or thirdly, as a regenerative tool or structure, to regenerate a disused brownfield site. Loosely speaking, there were two generations of flat blocks in central Dublin's twentieth-century history – the renowned and longstanding 1930s/1940s blocks designed by the Corporation's new Housing Architecture Department and the Housing Architect, Herbert Simms, and then the maisonette blocks from the late 1950s which proliferated across the inner city through the 1960s and into the 1970s.[6]

Though dogged and persistent, flats have always been differentiated, becoming problematically ghettoised homes in the experience of the city. Physically, flats represented closer continuity with stigmatised slum tenement housing. Emotionally, flats brought an element of individual space but always within the communal situation of a flat block. That communality, resilient communities, I argue, frightened and continues to frighten Irish housing officials. The rise of the individual over the collective might be a hallmark of Irish social history in the twentieth century. And housing, as society's most concrete output or product, followed suit. Summarising his late 1940s anthropological research on Irish urbanisation,

Alexander J. Humphreys observed that Irish society "tends to subordinate the group [...] to the individual."[7] He noted that while Dublin had experienced the agency of the labour union movement, generally it had developed as an individualist society, growing out of the "classical liberalism of nineteenth-century England rather than the socialism which stems largely from Marx."[8] We might conclude that, as debased versions of British Garden Suburb principles combined with pro-rural Irish Catholic social teaching, estates of individual houses were bound to prevail in Irish culture. Compounding these influences were the pragmatics of economics (suburban houses were cheaper) and slum clearance imperatives.

Part III: Class relations — lodgers, tenements and back to the flats

Irish cities, all cities, are expressed and defined by their houses and homes. And all homes have been influenced by issues of class. While slum clearance prompted the great swathes of housing estates from the 1940s onwards, littering Irish city edges in the present world, earlier industrial or colonial shifts underpinned the shaping of residential squares, urban villages and utopian schemes. In the lofty name of improvement or the lowly name of shelter, building modes like terraced housing emerged. The more economic and structurally beneficial sharing of walls enabled a rash spread of housing, coincident with industrialisation and new railways. Social stratification and housing history are long-time bedfellows. This, then, is much more enduring than a twentieth-century story. Consider the redbrick developments in Dublin's inner suburb of Drumcondra which appeared as domestic solutions for men (people) of, according to the Dublin Builder "moderate means [...] who spend the whole week in gloomy offices ... [and] would gladly select their habitation in some airy and beautiful locality, apart from the din that assails their ears during business hours."[9] The development of houses in the 1860s was a class-driven endeavour, motivated by the growing clerical population.

In that same suburb, the practice of renting a room to a lodger or a boarder had become commonplace by the time of the famous 1911 Census. Of the 532 individuals living on one such redbrick street, Hollybank Road, 45 were lodgers (i.e. 8.5%), while 17 of the 96 houses on that road (i.e. about 18%) accommodated lodgers. Presenting this social phenomenon in a recent study, historical geographer Ruth McManus uncovers the prevalence of lodging and boarding in Irish urban history. Almost forgotten and barely recorded, the practice of lodging, from the late nineteenth century and across most of the twentieth century, ultimately arose out of class concerns and housing costs. McManus analyses electoral rolls to discover the patterns of longstanding subtenancy in Dublin such as the example, among many in Drumcondra, of Edward J. Walker, a 51-year-old compositor from County Carlow who lived with the O'Neill family on Lindsay, later Crawford, Road. The O'Neills comprised 47-year-old teacher, Annie, and her retired teacher brother, John (69 years) along with their servant, Mary Anne Brady (30 years).[10] Evidently Walker stayed with the family during their change of address, pointing to the longer-term nature of his lodging. Or look at Ellen Dwyer, a tobacconist on Capel Street who accommodated four male lodgers – a shopman, a groom, a carpenter and a coachman. Therein lie just two portraits of diverse, but perhaps typical, early-twentieth-century Dublin households.

Dublin's lodgers primarily contributed to the rent or mortgage on a home, but often their contribution enabled a family to keep a servant. Lodgers and their hosts were often connected by geography (they were from the same rural place originally), or by employment (they worked together), or by religion, for which we might read 'ethnic background' in the Irish context. Some lodgers occupied unfurnished rooms; some paid for their board annually, and others by the week. Advertisements for lodgers were placed in daily newspapers with host households defining themselves as 'gentleman's family' or 'clergyman's widow' or 'good social position'. But one pattern emerging in this multi-various situation is that many homes with lodgers had widows and single women at the helm. Is this then a women's history? If nothing else, it is a socially stratified hidden history of home.

Astoundingly, one person in every twenty was a lodger in 1911 Dublin. As we know from our research into tenement Dublin, lodgers even infiltrated the tenement home.[11] Who would believe that an already unbearably overcrowded one or two-roomed family home might accommodate an extra adult? But again, the census and electoral roll evidence reluctantly and contradictorily mounts. In the worst slum areas of Mabbot Street for instance, a family of eight people in a two-roomed home had two adult male lodgers! Dublin's tenements, much like their Limerick and Cork counterparts, proliferated with the subdivision of fine Georgian town houses. As Patrick Abercrombie, British town-planner and author of London and Dublin's early twentieth-century city plans, famously asserted, Dublin had "the most architectural slums in the world."[12]

Here were brick terraced houses, four storeys high with simple floor plans of one room at the front, one room at the back and fireplaces in the party wall on one side only. These single-family mansions were ultimately flexible. And as Irish urbanisation took off, more as a consequence of rural depopulation than of Irish industrialisation, these houses became prime locations for speculating landlords. Soon, by the turn of the twentieth century, streets and streets of former houses of the gentry had been transformed into multi-household slum neighbourhoods, teeming with children. Large single rooms would house an entire family. Stacked and lacking in indoor sanitation, tenement homes were accessed by a shared front door, hall and stairway. This was a communal way of living and the hall and stairs,

Figure 6, Tenement Over Mantle,
Mrs Dowling's Flat (reconstruction),
14 Henrietta Street, 2018. Photograph
by Charles Duggan, Heritage
Officer, Dublin City Council

Figure 7, Lady of the Rock,
Dublin Windows, 2020.
Photograph by Paul Tierney

with the always-open front door becoming a semi-public ambiguous space, were a reluctant commons.

Tenement hallways were precarious and un-surveilled places; there was no light, stairs were missing bannisters, children fell, slops dripped down the treads and odours overwhelmed. So when the flats were built as an alternative to the tenement slums from 1932, the new schemes contained no internal corridors. Circulation was expelled to the outside of blocks and a culture of surveillance prevailed. Sanitation was hugely improved, with each new flat having its own indoor toilet as well as a metal bath under the scullery table. But most pointedly for our story of housing and class, each unit had its own front door and its own set of windows. Where, in the tenement room, the mantel over the usually massive fireplace was the site for decorative flourishes including family heirlooms and religious statuettes (Figure 6), the flat's windowsills became that new place to show and tell. Flourishes of pride and badges of ownership or occupation, windows could communicate much. After all, while a tenement household was lucky to have one window, a flat, or better still a house in a new suburban estate, had several views out onto the world beyond — all marking the triumph of the individual over the collective.

• And so... the Lady on the Rock

Most recently, and for about a decade, Dublin's working-class windows have played host to that alluring plaster cast statuette, the 'Lady on the Rock'. Window after window across Dublin has brandished this figure, with her mostly-naked body in profile, her head resolute and her athletic leg bare, interrupted artfully by a flowing garment (Figure 7 and 8). Regardless of housing type within the portfolio of working-class neighbourhoods, she has appeared in the windows of flats, and in the windows of terraced houses. Many wondered about her origin, about her place, as she became ubiquitous. Did she signal something untoward? Was she a status symbol?[13] Or was she a direct descendent of the tenement house, where a household could now, in the Dublin of 2020, lay claim to more than one window spread over two floors of a home? In the end, the 'Lady on the Rock' was 'just' a Dublin trend. She was an aesthetic choice and her prevalence pointed, ultimately, to complex and insoluble issues of taste and class; or to what Pierre Bourdieu might term, 'cultural capital'. Why did our neighbours have a 'Lady on the Rock' at every window, when we put terracotta-potted cacti in ours (Figure 9)? Why did our neighbours save their money for glitter walls - an all-new silky glittery plaster adorning homes all over inner-city Dublin - while we saved for a high-end British stove? Seemingly, the domestic realm, where our taste flourishes untamed, is a final bastion of class distinction. With these questions, I was reminded of Grayson Perry's artistic urge to comprehend the ethics beneath aesthetic taste. Underpinning his practice, most especially *The Vanity of Small Differences tapestry series* (2012), is this heady exploration of class and taste. In juxtaposing two of these tapestries, *The Adoration of the Cage Fighters and The Annunciation of the Virgin Deal*,[14] I uncomfortably recognised myself and my neighbour in our caricatured states: the former, a working-class domestic depiction where the mother, with gold hoop earrings, holds the baby with a soother away from her can of Red Bull and packet of cigarettes. In the Virgin Deal then, the middle-class figures stand by their Aga stove. The mantlepiece horse has been replaced by Penguin literary series mugs, and the un-self-conscious cigarettes by fresh organic vegetables, apparently carelessly laid out on the kitchen table.

From flat block to cottage, window sill to mantlepiece, housing frames all human life. Choices are limited. That's a historic fact. By the time of Ireland's slum clearance projects through the mid-twentieth century, housing had become dominated by greenfield development, extending the parameters of Irish cities for individual homes. While the appetite was for tradition and homogeneity, in reality, the suburban housing estate was a curious battleground between individual freedom and collective living. Ecologically reckless and demographically homogenous, Irish housing estates are probably most recognisable as places of single-class domestic life. As the most desirable housing type, their proliferation reflects a long housing-class history, which, in the end, is a history of aspiration and the allocation of scarce resources.

Figure 9, Cacti in Terracotta Pots.
Photograph by author, 2020

1. Evaristo, B. (2020). *Girl, Woman, Other*. Penguin Books, p.150–151.

2. Ibid., p.159.

3. Through a study of immigrants to Birmingham accessing housing, the concept of housing class emerged. Housing class definition: Scott, J. (ed.). (2014). *Dictionary of Sociology*. Oxford University Press.

4. Department of Local Government. (1943). *Enquiry into the Housing of the Working Classes*. Dublin: Stationery Office.

5. Anon. (1952, April 25). Houses or Flats. *The Irish Times*, p.5.

6. These two strong and distinguishable types were of course pre-empted by fairly isolated instances of flat blocks, provided either by philanthropic concerns (like Guinness), by the Dublin Artisan Dwelling Company, or indeed, by Dublin Corporation from the 1870s through the turn of the last century. For examples of these 1930s/1940s flat schemes around Dublin, see Oliver Bond House near the River Liffey in Dublin 7, or Greek Street's St Michan's flats and Chancery House scheme behind the Four Courts, also Dublin 7. See Henrietta House behind Henrietta Street (Dublin 1) and Pearse House, off Pearse Street in Dublin 2.

7. Humphreys, A.J. (1966). *New Dubliners: Urbanization and the Irish Family*. Routledge & Kegan Paul, p.29.

8. Ibid., p.29.

9. Anon. (1964, March 15). *Dublin Builder*.

10. McManus, R. (2018, December). Dublin's Lodger Phenomenon in the Early Twentieth Century. *Irish Economic and Social History* 45(1), p. 43.

11. 14 Henrietta Street, Dublin Tenement Museum, curatorial development from 2016–2018 undertaken by Dublin City Council Heritage Office and UCD Architecture/ Irish Research Council Fellowship.

12. Paraphrase of: Abercrombie, P. (1942, June). The Dublin Town Plan. *Studies*, p. 155–160. See also Abercrombie, P., Kelly, S. and Kelly, A. (1922). *Dublin of the Future. The New Town Plan*. Liverpool/London: University Press of Liverpool/Hodder + Stoughton with the Civics Institute of Ireland.

13. Ward, J. (Director). (2010). Lady on the Rock [short documentary film]. Darklight Film Festival 2010.

14. Perry, G. (2012). *The Vanity of Small Differences* tapestry series.

Further References

Campbell, H. (2020, February). *Houses in Motion* [radio broadcast]. Davis Now lecture, broadcast from Nano Nagle Centre, RTÉ Radio One.

Galavan, S. (2017). *Dublin's Bourgeois Homes: Building the Victorian Suburbs, 1850–1901*. Routledge.

McInerney, L. (2015). *Glorious Heresies*. John Murray Books.

Rowley, E. (2019). *Housing, Architecture and the Edge Condition*. Routledge.

ON FREE
THOUGHT FM

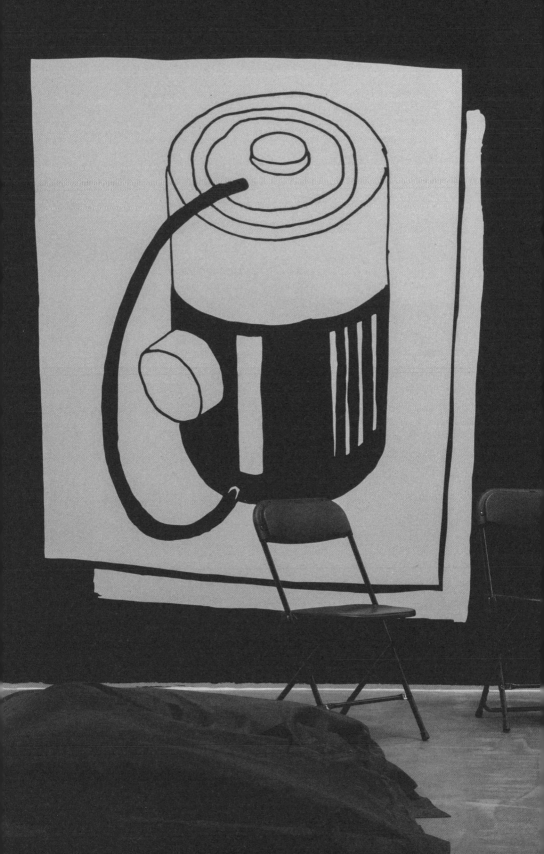

105.2FM: 'THIS CONVERSATION IS AN ARTWORK'[1]

I can't manage to get excited over politics, and these days a discourse that is not impassioned can't be heard, quite simply. There's a decibel threshold that must be crossed for discourse to be heard. And I don't cross it. Politics is not necessarily just talking, it can also be listening. Perhaps we lack a practice of listening and attention.

— Roland Barthes, in conversation with Henry Levi Strauss[2]

The question detailed above, of what is heard and how it is heard, resonates with Garrett Phelan's *FREE THOUGHT FM*, a radio-based art project that explores class inequality and access to education in the Greater Dublin area. Over a period of 30 days in 2019, Phelan used terrestrial radio broadcast as a space to discuss 'free thought' with invited guests and members of the public. The licensed station was temporarily located in the Douglas Hyde, a contemporary art gallery that is in turn housed within the walls of the University of Dublin, Trinity College.

A project that was nearly two years in the making, *FREE THOUGHT FM* builds on the artist's longstanding use of broadcast radio as a medium, and in particular on the 2016 project *HEED FM*. In this temporary 28-day broadcast, Phelan used radio to produce a portrait of individuals and groups of all backgrounds aged 18–25 to explore and articulate the hopes and aspirations of young Dubliners in the Greater Dublin area. Through research for *HEED FM* and the conversations that emerged, he became increasingly aware of the cultural and financial differences that foreclosed access to higher education for people in working-class areas. *FREE THOUGHT FM* centres this issue, drawing together conversations about education and class as these phenomena play out in Dublin.

The exhibition had three separate aspects. Within the walls of the Douglas Hyde was the radio station itself, where speakers were invited to explore a range of topics relating to class inequality and access to education. On these walls were hung vinyl replicas of Phelan's process-driven drawings for the project. The second aspect was the broadcast signal, which radiated beyond the gallery into the city in the form of FM waves. Finally, a visual marketing campaign, across social media and 100 IPA billboard poster sites throughout the city, used print and digital advertising avenues to share straightforward information about topics such as the CAO[3] process and grants for higher-level education. Alongside this visual marketing campaign, an outreach programme saw 'Alternative Routes to Education' booklets distributed at the gallery and to DEIS[4] schools.

Over 30 days the artist spoke to educators, students, community organisations, activists, advocates and representative groups across the political and community spectrum. Speakers were invited to talk about their experience of education. Matters of concern included people's experiences and the resulting conversations (available as an archive online)[5] move seamlessly between the personal and the political; individual socio-economic factors that limited or facilitated speakers' ability to access education, and their feelings about education and personal worth, are explored alongside the broader systemic arrangements of access and exclusion as they play out in the Greater Dublin area. Ultimately, the questions explored hinge on how to make those things that are nominally free, that supposedly 'everyone knows about/can apply for/can participate in', more actually accessible. If there's a specific ambition to draw attention to resources and routes to third-level education, therefore, there's also a more generic ambition to point to and unpick a whole set of economic, cultural and social power asymmetries as they play out in institutions like the media, the city, the university and the gallery space.

Phelan effectively manned the radio station for six days a week but he was not by any means the only voice shaping the discussion. The project was carefully designed in collaboration with Michelle Kinsella, adult and community education officer at the National University of Ireland, Maynooth, and a key facilitator of *HEED FM*. It was also shaped by a diverse group of facilitators and co-hosts that included researchers, social activists, artists and educators. Among these were David Joyce, Calvin Darcy-Kanda, Shane Brothwood, Sophie Mullervey and Tamara Harawa, who themselves spoke as part of the broadcast and who were also invited to engage with guests to the station. The Douglas Hyde team were also involved in the day-to-day running of the broadcast, welcoming visitors and speaking with them about the social issues at the heart of the show. Visitors could also participate in the radio broadcasts.

What does it mean to position a contemporary art gallery nested in a prestigious university as the antenna for these public discussions? What kinds of exclusions and foreclosures does this notion of the public assume? And might broadcast, sound and listening offer ways of reconfiguring publics, nurturing a public space or otherwise drawing people together?

• **What does it mean to make things public?**

I worked as a tour guide in Dublin City Gallery The Hugh Lane straight out of art college. A typical day consisted of guiding tours of primary school children, Leaving Certificate art students and English language students around the public gallery. On one end of the 'public' spectrum were teenage boys from Dublin's most expensive private schools who called me ironically by my first name, while on the other end were schools or youth outreach groups slated in advance as 'disadvantaged' or 'with behavioural problems'. If the former moved through the gallery space as casually as they might have stepped through their own living room in socked feet, the latter usually asked my permission just to stand there and look at a painting by Jack B. Yeats. Phelan is careful to acknowledge that his own experience of both education and cultural institutions is different from that of the groups that *FREE THOUGHT FM* worked to engage with. The artist came of age in Dublin in the 1970s and 80s as a student at the fee-paying boys' school

Belvedere College, an establishment that's notable for its arts alumni – writer James Joyce, artist Harry Clarke, and art historian, curator and Director of the National Gallery of Ireland (1927–1935) Thomas Bodkin – and for its work in the local communities. Phelan describes visiting the Douglas Hyde as a student of Belvedere on a school trip and later returning by himself on weekend trips. He was actively encouraged to enter public cultural institutions and feel like he belonged there. *FREE THOUGHT FM* arises from a keen desire to use radio and broadcast media to make public resources like culture and education more universally accessible, to foster a genuine sense that "anyone can and should come into this space."[6]

The project engages with the history of radio as an idealised public space, using the terrestrial broadcast as a virtual space where publics can rapidly form and disperse. But in its particular use of radio and sound, it also challenges understandings of how these publics are made. For example, German sociologist Jürgen Habermas' 'public sphere' describes a virtual or physical gathering that comes together through discussion about matters of shared concern to that community. For Habermas, this discursive space was 'open to all',[7] a non-hierarchical, inclusive arena for discussion that could foment political action and lead to social change. Habermas' theorisations of the public sphere have come under criticism for emphasising discursive acts over other non-linguistic ways of participating in politics and for failing to recognise the exclusions (social, economic, cultural, identity) implicit in the supposedly 'inclusive' or 'common' spaces they describe.[8] What other ways and through what other acts might publics come together and disperse? What kinds of barriers exist to participation in public? And what role can the medium of radio play in forming publics and, following on from this, political action?

Making things public becomes a central part of the process of *FREE THOUGHT FM*. The project does this in two ways. First, through conversations, Phelan uses the broadcast to ask what is inside and outside of the public remit. Who gets to participate? Who has access to ostensibly public resources like education, information or communications? In using a licensed radio station to explore the implicit ways in which access to universal services is foreclosed to certain groups, it brings these unspoken exclusions to the fore. It questions who has access to education, who is excluded and what systems perpetuate inequality. Who is willing to and able to contribute? Situated in a contemporary art gallery in an elite university, this conversation isn't without its own tensions, but this static is part of the broadcast rather than something to be silenced. Furthermore, through its visual marketing campaign, realised physically across the city and digitally on social media, the project works to reach an audience that might not visit the gallery space. Indeed, working with youth marketing company Thinkhouse was an integral part of the development of the project.

The second way *FREE THOUGHT FM* reconfigures the public is through the medium of sound and radio waves. Phelan asks us to pay attention not only to the messages relayed over the airwaves but also to the physical properties of sound and radio. *FREE THOUGHT FM* challenges dominant conceptions of the public sphere by using not only discourse, but also the physicality of the wavelength to enact its publics.

• **Sonic publics**

Audio cultures have more recently explored how sound events might help to constitute a public space and draw people together. Writing of acoustic arenas, Barry Blesser and Linda-Ruth Salter explore how sonic events and their interlocutors create a shared sense of community and belonging.[9] The acoustic arena can be defined as the shared social space in which a sonic event is made audible. This arena has "invisible boundaries based on aural experience rather than on tangible physical surfaces"[10] and it is naturally inclusive; an individual who broadcasts there makes a sonic connection to everyone in that area. These acts might be linguistic, like a radio or loudspeaker voice broadcast, but they are just as often natural, industrial or percussive.

Blesser and Salter argue further that cues about the openness/inclusivity of a space can be intimated through its acoustic architecture. Sound communicates the cultural and social meanings of a space. These might be overt, such as the 'mosquito' tones designed to discourage young people idling outside a shopping centre, or they might be more subtle – the way a voice reverberates or is muted by a surface, the footsteps of a security guard on a marble floor, the anechoic hush of the white cube gallery space. Furthermore, a class composition underpins the composition of the public soundscape.[11] Particular sounds get characterised as 'noise' – foreign languages, certain accents, the sound of music played through a tinny phone speaker on public transport, private residential sounds leaking from an open window onto a street. Similarly, while radio's acoustic arena is often presented as the ultimate public space, a conduit that transgresses physical borders and offers expansive contact, state and/or commercial interests often structure the terms of entry and participation.

FREE THOUGHT FM introduces us to its own acoustic arena. Tuning in online or via FM radio we can listen to the stories being told, but we also immediately hear the reverberant space of the Douglas Hyde, the sound of a large room, sparsely furnished with vinyl prints on the walls, some basic radio equipment, and beanbags and folding chairs for free thinkers and listeners. Alongside the voices of our speakers, which are front and centre, we also hear the muted sounds of visitors moving in and around the gallery during the broadcast. In lulls in the conversation, the familiar sounds of the city bleed into the gallery space – footfall moving through the Nassau street entrance to the university, distant traffic, the chime of the Luas as it turns right onto Dawson Street.

Theorists such as Salome Voeglin and Brandon LaBelle both explore the role of sound as a medium for tactical resistance, an acoustic space reverberating with the possibility of reclaiming political agency; they're concerned with the scope of sound to upset a politics of the public sphere based on 'appearance' and visibility to one another – a space for blind address.[12]

These ideas have long been in Garrett Phelan's work and *FREE THOUGHT FM* **takes them up directly. The 30-day transmission engages with the voice as a discursive medium, exploring wide-ranging topics from inequality in education to sound, radio, space and class. Phelan wants to engage a diversity of different voices and accents, challenging the traditional protocols and politics of predominantly middle-class arenas such as the public radio broadcast, the art gallery and the university.**

But the broadcast also transcends discourse, because the voice proceeds from the body and brings the body into relation with the outside world. The voices of the invited speakers carry a lot of extra information beyond the words they speak – where and when they grew up, whether English is their first language. There are hints in little awkward pauses or in conspiratorial laughter that tell us how well each speaker knows the artist. Some of the voices we hear are confident, clearly comfortable speaking aloud in a public forum, while others are more hesitant, even apologetic.

FREE THOUGHT FM **explores not only the politics of sound and the voice, but also the politics of terrestrial radio as a wavelength, as electromagnetic vibrations that interact with, and sometimes even restructure, the situations they encounter.**

- Radio publics

Phelan has outlined that radio, a medium he uses frequently in his work, is a permanent monument, a signal that travels forever. Radio interacts with the surrounding architecture; electromagnetic waves are attenuated and absorbed by their surroundings and mould themselves to spaces. The radio station on the frequency of 105.2 FM provides a space for discourse about shared societal concerns, but it is also a sculptural medium, one that interacts as electromagnetic waves with the surrounding environment.[13] Waveforms play a role in the construction of our public spaces and sometimes underpin the terms of exclusion or access. But waves are also formless, vibratory, embodied; they transgress borders in subtle ways and reconfigure relationships to spaces and to each other. The history of radio art and activism is full of these signals, where waves are used to communicate across geographic borders or to draw listeners together and create molecular gatherings.[14]

When Phelan started working in radio in the early 1990s, pirate stations had been filtered out by the introduction of community and education licences that were made available by the Independent Radio and

Television Commission (IRTC), now the Broadcasting Authority of Ireland. Phelan describes this moment as a "golden age for broadcasting",[15] when many stations dropped the 'pirate' tag because they were recognised and legitimised by the coalitions in place at the time. Phelan engages not only with questions of equality and access, and radio as a public medium, but also radio as part of the bureaucratic institutions that govern and structure discourse in a public space. Instead of structuring the station as a digital broadcast or a transgressive pirate broadcast, all of Phelan's radio stations deliberately engage with the architecture of public communications. This is no easy feat and involved engaging with the Broadcasting Authority of Ireland (BAI) to obtain a temporary radio licence, demonstrating that the work was not only ratified by the State but also in the public interest. As with all of Phelan's previous radio stations, the commissioning institution of *FREE THOUGHT FM*, the Douglas Hyde, applied for a temporary licence on the artist's behalf in order to receive an FM bandwidth frequency for the 30-day broadcast. *FREE THOUGHT FM* deliberately engages with the infrastructures that structure access to communications, in other words, working from inside this space rather than outside of it. Of course, any claims for doing things 'in public' or creating an inclusive space need to be carefully considered. Communication doesn't equal community and the airwaves are not inherently open to everyone, but radio art and radio activism have historically been a place for troubling these exclusions.

As with his interest in exclusion and access in education, Phelan is also interested in the power dynamics of radio, in who gets to speak and have a voice, in what is represented and what is omitted. It is tempting to frame this as a hierarchical structure where a privileged few get to have a voice in shaping the public conversation, but from its inception *FREE THOUGHT FM* worked to give over ownership of these public spaces.

In one conversation with social activist Calvin D'arcy Kanda, Phelan acknowledges his own position of privilege but explains that his approach, alongside thorough research, is to open dialogue with these communities and their interlocutors, to constantly ask for feedback, criticism and input from the groups and individuals he is working to engage with.[16]

The radio format bears some similarity to public service broadcasting, with its short conversational segments, but the similarities, from the topics discussed to the invited speakers, end there. Traditionally, public service broadcasting is beholden both to partisan interests and/or to advertising revenue to fund programming. The result is often that programming follows a uniform model with content that is acceptable to advertisers and/or state actors. This often means that a select few shape the content while everyone else is encouraged to be a fairly passive listener. Experimental or critical content is often limited. *FREE THOUGHT FM* subverts this model by experimenting not only with a more critical, active and inclusive form of radio content and conversation, but also with a more critical, active and engaged form of listening.

Alongside discussions of access to education, Phelan poses a larger question and asks listeners to consider more broadly what education is and should be in the future. The pedagogy of *FREE THOUGHT FM* isn't about producing some kind of dawning awareness in an invisible mass of disadvantaged or uneducated listeners that eventually leads to political or social action. Instead, by creating a space for conversation and collective listenership, it works to change who has a voice, what can be said and who is counted in public spaces.[17] This is how *FREE THOUGHT FM* makes new publics – it shows us that listening to popular media can be more than a training course in passivity, as Adorno described it.[18] It can also be a quiet sabotage of the institutions and technologies used to underpin class exclusion, with their own instruments.[19] Here, Roland Barthes' statement that "politics is not necessarily just talking, it can also be listening",[20] has a new resonance.

Endnotes

1. Georgina Jackson in conversation with Garrett Phelan at the inaugural broadcast of *FREE THOUGHT FM*. Available at: https://freethoughtfm.bandcamp.com/track/day-1-dr-georgina-jackson-the-douglas-hyde-gallery.

2. Barthes, R. (2009). *The Grain of the Voice: Interviews 1962–1980*. Northwestern University Press.

3. The Central Applications Office (CAO) processes applications for undergraduate courses in Irish higher education institutions.

4. DEIS, or Delivering Equality of Opportunity in Schools, identifies the Department of Education and Skills' national programme to address educational disadvantage throughout the public school system.

5. The archive is available at https://freethoughtfm.bandcamp.com/.

6. Garrett Phelan, in conversation with director Georgina Jackson at the inaugural broadcast of *FREE THOUGHT FM*. Available at: https://freethoughtfm.bandcamp.com/track/day-1-dr-georgina-jackson-the-douglas-hyde-gallery.

7. Habermas, J. (1991). *The Structural Transformation of the Public Sphere: An Inquiry into a Category of Bourgeois Society*. MIT Press.

8. Fraser, N. (1990). Rethinking the public sphere: A contribution to the critique of actually existing democracy. *Social Text 25/26*: pp. 56–80; Warner, M. (2002). Publics and counterpublics. *Public Culture 14*(1): pp. 49–90.

9. Blesser, B. and Salter, L.R. (2009). *Spaces Speak, Are You Listening?: Experiencing Aural Architecture*. MIT Press.

10. Blesser, B. and Salter, L.R. (1995). Eventscapes: the aural experience of space. *Mental 101*: p.94.

11. Thompson, E.A. (2004). *The Soundscape of Modernity: Architectural Acoustics and the Culture of Listening in America, 1900–1933*. MIT Press; Bijsterveld, K. (2008). *Mechanical Sound: Technology, Culture, and Public Problems of Noise in the Twentieth Century*. MIT Press.

12. See for example: Voegelin, S. (2018). *The Political Possibility of Sound: Fragments of Listening*. Bloomsbury Publishing USA; and, LaBelle, B. (2018). Sonic Agency: Sound and Emergent Forms of Resistance. Vol. 1. MIT Press.

13. Mann, L.K. (2019). Sonic publics| Booming at the margins: Ethnic radio, intimacy, and nonlinear innovation in media. *International Journal of Communication 13*: p. 19.

14. Take, for example, practices such as offshore pirate stations, border blasting or artistic experiments such as Tetsuo Kogawa's work with mini FM.

15. Garrett Phelan, in conversation with the author, 7 January 2020.

16. Garrett Phelan, in conversation with Calvin D'arcy Kanda. Available at: https://freethoughtfm.bandcamp.com/track/day-5-calvin-darcy-kanda.

17. This is what Jacques Rancière would call 'the distribution of the sensible'. For Rancière, art is politically effective not because it teaches its audiences what to think about political issues, but because it can transform what he calls 'the distribution of the sensible', changing who has a voice, who is counted in a political sphere, and also what can be thought and said about a particular topic. In: Rancière, J. (2004). *The Politics of Aesthetics: The Distribution of the Sensible*. Continuum.

18. Adorno's description of popular music in America is as a "training course in passivity that will probably spread to [the listener's] thought and social conduct". In: Adorno, T. (1989). *Introduction to the Sociology of Music*. New York: Continuum, p. 30.

19. Chow, R. (1990). Listening otherwise, music miniaturized: a different type of question about revolution. *Discourse 13*(1): p. 148.

20. Barthes, R. (2009). *The Grain of the Voice: Interviews 1962–1980*. Northwestern University Press.

IN
CONVERSATION:
ON FREE
THOUGHT FM

Georgina Jackson: *FREE THOUGHT FM* was multi-faceted: a 30-day live radio broadcast, on the airwaves across Dublin and online, which invited artists, academics, community and youth groups, and activists, amongst others, to talk with you and the other hosts live from the installation of your drawings across the walls of the gallery; a youth-focused marketing campaign over 100 billboard sites across the city, and across social media; a booklet giving 'hacks' to routes to education and support systems which was available online, at the gallery and sent to DEIS [Delivering Equality of Opportunity in Schools] schools in Dublin; and a series of talks in schools with artists, sportspeople and politicians, speaking about their own experiences of education, as well as talks in the gallery, one of which looked at Leaving Certificate reform. How did this expansive project begin? And how did the questions around access and education emerge within your work?

Garrett Phelan: *HEED FM* [1] [2016] was an independent radio station, an artwork in the form of a radio soundwork that was an anonymous portrait of young people aged 18 to 25 living in the Greater Dublin Area. I was looking at young people 100 years after the Easter Rising, the revolution within Ireland. It was a celebratory, centenary project funded by the Arts Council and I spent several years with my team and with many contributors creating that portrait. *HEED FM* raised a lot of issues for myself, the team and those that contributed to it. When focussing on the aspirations and passions of young people in detail we soon realised how the system in place largely prevents these young people from achieving their aspirations or realising their dreams. It's a system that is unequal. Of course we say this daily, we hear others say it, but when you have a conversation with someone who experiences it, and you talk about their aspirations in depth, you hear them describe with passion what they want to do in life, but you also hear how there are huge social barriers for them to overcome in achieving that – well, it's very different. So I had questions that came out of *HEED FM*, and then your invitation to exhibit in the Douglas Hyde was the first thing that sparked *FREE THOUGHT FM* really. There was suddenly the possibility of a platform to put those questions and issues arising from *HEED* out there in a public way. These questions were around access to education, class inequality and issues surrounding education. Advocacy doesn't exist and certainly didn't exist at that time for young people 18 to 25 who were having difficulties in their social environment and the huge question of class inequality in the city made itself all too apparent through *HEED FM*.

Georgina: *HEED FM* was unique – hearing young people talk at length about the things that they were passionate about, their hopes, and the things that they wanted to see happen in their lives. This lasting portrait captured so much, nothing like the 'sound bites' usually heard in the media. And one of the conversations we had at an early point in *FREE THOUGHT FM* was the issue of access to education for young people, and how, through *HEED*, it became so visible that there were monumental barriers to this.

Garrett: Yes, and I think the significant factor here is that The Douglas Hyde is situated within the Trinity College campus and Trinity College is the most historically elitist educational institution in Ireland. What it stood for and stands for as a symbol in the city, which you can see reflected in its architecture, its enclosed space with high railings around it, is indicative of how the city operated in the past and continues to operate today. The university has obviously changed over many years to be more welcoming and to be more open and inclusive but you can still feel the physical and psychological barriers, the obstacles to self-development and education for all. That awareness of Trinity as a context was a significant factor in what we were about to undertake.

HEED FM actually started out as a project looking at the homelessness crisis and ended up being about young people in general. They are the ones who no one caters for. And young people are the most misrepresented people on media platforms. At that point in time in our research, they were always presented negatively. There were awful documentaries being made about Sheriff Street, which is an important, historical working-class part of Dublin city, but it's always portrayed in the media in the negative, as are many other areas of Dublin. This became all too clear to me in the making of *HEED FM*. Again, we know this, we have grown up with it, we are saturated by it, but therefore we are immune to it and as a result we prefer to ignore it. So when I came face to face with this kind of prejudice, it was unacceptable to me.

I started the process of looking at it through my own experience and the experience of others on the team, using being young and growing up in Dublin as a reference point. For me, it's not all about where you go wrong, it's also about where you go right and about what you're dreaming of and what you want to do with your life. How can you contribute? What are your aspirations? So why should the focus of a project not be on those positive things? Also, I was conscious that there were a couple of significant people in my life who helped me achieve things because I didn't get a Leaving Certificate. Even though I went to a very privileged school, I still didn't get the qualification at the end. And although going to that school really helped me, there were still barriers and major obstacles for me to overcome. Fortunately, I was savvy enough to seek out significant people who helped me break through those barriers because I was able to ask them for help. But not everybody is like that, not everybody has the confidence or feels they have the right to ask certain people for help. Most people believe what they're being told with certainty, that if they don't get the Leaving Certificate, they will not go forward and they will not get to do or achieve the things they want to do in life. That if they fail, the only direction for them is existing on the very bottom rung. Their aspirations are cut. There have to be other paths, and there are, to achieving your hopes.

The word 'access' is about being open, but much of the information about access to education is hidden, is buried, and I became very aware of that during *HEED FM*. You have to dig deep to find official help and specific questions emerged for me, such as, why is the government not investing money into communicating these pathways? Making it clear and simple? And these pathways really are hidden, even today. The SUSI grant system,[2] the DARE system,[3] the HEAR system,[4] these are hidden supports that parents and students must dig through layers of bureaucracy to find. It could be through a chance conversation with a guidance counsellor, if you have one, that you'll discover that you might be able to receive assistance to afford third-level education or another form of education, and to access it. When people don't know about this, they might automatically refuse their children the option and students might refuse themselves the right to education because of the family financial situation. There is also a stigma attached to funding assistance. And this is a massive failure on the part of successive governments. This is wrong. We should all feel we can go to a third-level college or into other forms of further education if we want to.

The system of governance in Ireland is highly bureaucratic. This is what we have put in place. You have a lot of people who work in the public sector who want to help, but they're also hampered by the procedural systems. There is no fast easy access route. There's lots of paperwork that stops them from making this information more readily available to people. So, that was the problem we attempted to address – how to make that information more visible and available? We decided to try and offer a small solution: *FREE THOUGHT FM*. We also looked at the apprenticeship system and we looked at other alternative routes through education. We asked the question: what actually is education? Is it based purely on rote learning, or does life experience matter too? I suppose what was to the fore here was an exposé of the traditional concept and understanding of what education is and of what third-level education is and how we arrive there from primary and secondary level.

Georgina: One of your guests on *FREE THOUGHT FM* was feminist, activist and academic Ailbhe Smyth, who talked about the importance of education "not as a space to press us down or to put a lid on us." She argued that education as constraint must be replaced with education as a space for what "a person needs to be flourishing as a full human being, where your human capacities have the chance to grow and flourish, to lead a life with a sense of dignity." She highlighted that, "How we think? What we think? Why we think? Who gets to think more than other people? … are really the questions that define who and where we are in society."[5] What do education and free thought mean to you?

Garrett: The conversation with Ailbhe was important. Her words and experience made a big impression on me. I agree with everything she said. Education is free access to knowledge and experience to develop each individual person to the best of their capabilities. That's what it should be there for, to get the best out of every person and there should never, ever be any boundary or barrier to stop something like that experience. And any system that prevents that, tiered or otherwise, should be immediately dismantled. It should not exist. So, the way we're inducting our children right now into the current education system is wrong.

Georgina: Marshall McLuhan wrote that radio "comes to us ostensibly with person-to-person directness that is private and intimate, while in more urgent fact, it is really a subliminal echo chamber of magical power to touch remote and forgotten chords."[6] Radio was a key part of *FREE THOUGHT FM* and this medium in particular has been a crucial part of your practice, from A.A.R.T. - Radio (Audio Artists Radio Transmissions) in 1994, *Black Brain Radio* in 2006 to *HEED FM* in 2016. Indeed, one of the drawings in the gallery was of a radio you had when you were a teenager. Why is radio so important to you? Why do you return to it as a medium to work with?

Garrett: Well radio is like a gallery or paint or paper or a pencil. It's just another material or platform to communicate with. What interested me about using radio as an artform was that I see radio as both space and object. It can be a gallery or it can be a sculpture at the same time. It's democratic, it's open. There's no intimidation turning your radio on. You can access it almost anywhere, everybody has the right to it, and everybody knows that they have the right to it, that's the difference. Art galleries are public spaces but they are stigmatised by their history, designed and built for the public but mainly by the privileged for the privileged. They can be austere and I think austerity tends to speak to those that are wealthy, who believe that they have the right and privilege to access these places and the things that we see as ostentatious or grand or that improve their intellect, their sense of self-worth or that grant cultural capital. Radio as a space has less baggage. I think radio has a sense of commonality about it – the airwaves at one point were part of that idea of 'the common'. Interestingly, that word has a negative connotation in Dublin and in many other places – to be 'common' is to be somehow unrefined, implying you're 'lesser'. That was a word that influenced me in the making of this project. I think the fact that radio is democratic, open radio is democratic, open and accessible to all, makes it a very healthy environment. Or at least that is what it can be. Obviously a lot of what's on radio now is corporate-agenda-driven, run by the State or commercial enterprise. It is not a

free space because it's bound by guidelines and the law. However, if approached in the way that I have with *FREE THOUGHT FM*, these restrictions can be played with. That interests me, to challenge that with my radio works. But I feel it still has hidden potential as an alternative, less intimidating space to exhibit work and express ideas. That is why I engage with the space and the bureaucracy surrounding it. I still find it interesting to challenge the guidelines.

I have a long relationship with radio. It has always been a space that intrigued me. I've worked in many galleries, including IMMA [Irish Museum of Modern Art] in the 90s, where I worked with different types of artists from all over the world. It was a great education. We were really entering this new phase of contemporary art in Ireland at that time, a huge change was happening. We suddenly had a contemporary art museum and I was reading a lot of different books and meeting all of these new people from different parts of the planet. We were conversing in depth with these artists in very intense ways because we wanted to develop our language, the language of visual art. Working with sound as an artform became something that I really wanted to develop because I knew it didn't really exist in Ireland, but did in other cities in the world. So, I started up sound workshops with several other people and through the course of that I felt that an appropriately contextualised space for sound as an artform, the space to actually exhibit the work, was and is radio. Shortly after the workshops, I went about applying for a licence from the Broadcasting Authority of Ireland [BAI] and getting funding for a dedicated radio station. I applied and was awarded a small amount of funding for the project from the Arts Council, IMMA supported the project to a large degree and eventually I manage to succeed in receiving the licence from the BAI. I enjoyed the subversion of using institutional support to get the licence. It took a while and a lot of convincing of the right people, but it worked. This became the independent radio station A.A.R.T. - Radio⁽⁷⁾ back in '94 and it was part of an IMMA exhibition called *From Beyond the Pale*. One of a kind. We invited artists from all over the world to exhibit their work and so I really began to understand and appreciate the value of radio as another type of museum/gallery/curated space.

Georgina: As you say, you see possibility within radio that maybe doesn't exist in other forms – a certain type of openness that it possesses and its potential as a democratic space. You've also spoken about the physical qualities of radio. Can you tell me more about the way that you see and feel radio and the possibilities of these experiences?

Garrett: We can only qualify something we see by something we also cannot see, by something being invisible. We can't have a visual spectrum unless we have invisibility. Therefore, the soundwaves and electromagnetic wave particles and all of these things that carry sound that we can't see can be included in that spectrum. Now these qualify themselves as materials I can use, from the position of a visual artist. They are part of vision for me. I figured this out in my own way of thinking as a self-taught artist.

There is physicality to this energy, the invisible tangible. It touches us but we cannot feel it. We can, if we adjust volume levels through speakers, but electromagnetic waves pass through us. If I broadcast a signal from the Dublin Mountains, it travels from the mountain and out in this spherical invisible form. It resonates from this spherical shape and it hits the buildings and it hits the houses and it goes through the houses and it goes through our bodies. The signal goes out the other wall behind me and it heads off in that direction for as long as it can, as long as that punch of electrical power can send that signal. It is an incredibly powerful concept. I understand it as hugely physical. If used in a specific way and if I attach a meaning to that, that becomes sculpture for me. The less interruption, the farther the signal goes. The more power behind the signal the farther it goes. These are the physical properties that happen. That really excites me. I can do so much with that.

The other idea that really interests me is that the signal can travel forever, based on what we understand about it today. That meaning may change tomorrow. These interpretations and how I play with them become really important symbols for me. They illustrate meaning surrounding barriers, boundaries, difference and obstacles, or freedoms for that matter, in overcoming these barriers. Breaking through, going forward, going forever. These thoughts challenge our perceptions of time. That signal becomes a monument to me. In its own time it is contemporary. An everlasting monument. Always contemporary. Something that you make out of concrete or something that you make out of stone or wood or metal will last a certain amount of time. But this tiny signal will travel out into space in this circular motion – behind us, down through the ground, up into the sky, in all different directions, forever. So, it's an incredibly powerful symbol if we think of it in that way. Read in this way, the signal unravels notions of class, unravels illusions of grandeur, deconstructs this privilege of being educated. It changes our perception of time.

The commissioning process is simple for me really. You come to me, you say "I'd love you to do something with radio because I think it's a really interesting area and I want to challenge the function of the gallery". We create an independent FM radio station and that becomes the first part of it. This now potentially expands your audience radically. Your walls and roof and floor are irrelevant. Everybody who has a radio has access to your gallery, to your space. The gallery becomes ultra-democratic. Anyone can tune in. This is the form of the artwork and then the content comes later through the conversations that took place.

Georgina: You have also spoken about how people, individuals, have increasingly become part of your practice. *FREE THOUGHT FM* was developed with a number of different people including Michelle Kinsella and the staff at the marketing agency Thinkhouse, and realised with an expanded team including Shane Brothwood, Calvin D'arcy Kanda, Rachel Donnelly, Tamara Harawa, David Joyce, Sophie Mullervey and Aideen Quirke. Why was working with other people so central to the development of the project?

Garrett: In some cases other people are better able to relate to and communicate with others than I can. I have my limitations as someone who's in conversation with another person and I think I was very conscious and aware of that based on my previous experience with *HEED FM*. We needed other sounds, additional voices and life experiences. It's important to listen and make decisions from

there. One of the problems with radio is that there isn't a broad enough spectrum of voices on the airwaves. We need different accents from all genders, which span the broad cultural occupancy of the city. Presenters with different accents, reflecting the true diversity of the country we live in. These are simple issues that I felt needed to, and could be, easily addressed.

Georgina: The idea of working with a marketing agency was also very much part of the initial conversation about this project and they were an essential partner. Why engage a marketing agency as part of this artwork?

Garrett: In the art world, we have a very limited skills base in terms of how we market ourselves and our spaces, and under very restrained budgets. As an artist, I am very interested in this as part of my work. Our government has marketing departments, businesses have marketing departments, and when they have a product or an initiative and they want to let people know about it, they contract an advertising agency, a public relations consultant and a marketing expert to make sure that there's a strategy in place for the widest possible dissemination of the product/ initiative to ensure the highest and greatest public awareness around it. So, part of my artwork with *FREE THOUGHT FM* was to contract a marketing agency to be able to sell my concept. The simple concept was disseminating information on access to education to young people and to areas where people don't receive information on access to education or educational funding. We are attempting to rebalance things.

I contracted a youth branding marketing agency called Thinkhouse. We briefed the agency to focus specifically and only on districts that had the lowest rates of attendance to third-level colleges and we directly marketed information about alternative routes to funding and alternative routes to education to these demographics. We did this by creating a targeted social media campaign. We focused on young people who were 15 to 18 and hoped that Thinkhouse would have a lot of information on that age group and strategies in place for selling different brands to those young people and their parents. My idea was to apply the same marketing process as would be used for a brand, but just switch the product information. It's a very simple idea in one sense, but one that I hadn't seen before.

In the time after *HEED FM* I kept saying to myself and others, 'if you can sell someone Coca Cola or a new pair of trainers, surely you can "sell" the public information about accessing education in a simple, accessible way, information they want and need'. Dead simple, really easy and I never see it anywhere. I don't see aggressive campaigning on the part of successive governments in Ireland about ensuring that the entire youth population have a fair crack at getting access to all levels and types of education. I don't see them aggressively removing a system of class inequality and creating a system of fairness. So as part of the art we chose this approach.

Georgina: I like the idea of addressing a problem head on through marketing. If we can sell new trainers or an energy drink, why can't we sell important information?

Garrett: Whatever you're interested in, the information about it is there, it's in your face – most of it, useless products. There's a huge marketing push for a short period of time to feed the largest number of people possible. Businesses live in the hope that there is a viral reaction to their product and word of mouth attaches to it. So, this aspect of the project was an experiment to see if we could do the same, or at the very least illustrate this idea clearly, which I believe we did.

This work as art and radio expanded beyond the norms of what the art object is and what a gallery is, but fundamentally it is still an artwork, in its totality. For me it exists as a sculpture in many respects, with lots of different creative interventions, but still very much a sculpture.

Georgina: Over the 30 days of the broadcast you spoke with educators, geographers, sociologists, architectural historians, artists, musicians, actors, activists, students, youth workers, representatives from Pavee Point, the Irish Wheelchair Association, the Irish Refugee Council and many more. These conversations were never radio friendly sound bites but extended, deep, complex at times, vulnerable conversations about individuals' experience of education, the barriers that exist and the necessity, and ideas, for change. They would last 40 minutes, sometimes an hour and a half, and there was an emphasis on really digging deep. But also, there was a kind of vulnerability that existed both on your part and the guest's part. Why were these extended conversations so central to the project?

Garrett: It was vital to the project that we source experts and contributors who would be willing to contribute to the overall conversation in important ways. Anybody who is on radio, from any politician or any volunteer organisation rep to the average person, is usually given a few minutes to say what they need to say. For me, there's no depth in this process, there's no quality in it, there are no pregnant pauses in it, there's no natural thinking going on, there's no humanity in it. It's a very sound bite-y, sterile process, sexily driven. It's a very packaged process, it's about speed and drive, there's no calm, clean conversation or chat. No normality. It's unhealthy. With *FREE THOUGHT FM* and other stations that I have made, there is no adherence to normal programming structures. I have no advertising, no jingles, no time markers, no structure to it in the traditional sense. I wanted to give people time to think. We ran out of conversation a lot of the time. That's lovely. We ran out of talking, we exhausted the subject and that's a great thing to be able to do, it's a great luxury to have that.

The people that we spoke to I suppose had to tick a couple of boxes. Did they relate to the class inequality of Dublin City? Did they have an opinion on how the education system operates? Or what was their role in that and were they historians, were they human geographers, were they your average citizen? We also gave people the opportunity to volunteer to come in and speak to us, so it wasn't all about hand picking contributors. If someone suggested someone to us, we'd go and ask them. We had a pressure on us certainly to invite speakers who would answer the questions of class inequality in Dublin city: Why is it there? What are its origins and how can we change it? And then other question boxes to tick were: What's it like to do the Leaving Certificate? Does your future depend on the Leaving Certificate? Are there alternative routes to the Leaving Certificate? Can I access third-level education? If I come from a poor background, what is it

like in third-level education? How will it affect my life? How will it affect my family's life? All of these questions had to be answered. So, we researched heavily, drafted a list of questions and went in search of people to answer them. And that's why we have such an array of conversations, and what I believe to be a really important archive of information available on these questions and subjects. An archive which is available in perpetuity.

Georgina: The artwork spread far beyond the walls of the gallery, from the radio station broadcasting on 105.2FM, the digital broadcast online and the billboards up across the city, to the talks with transition and Leaving Certificate students in schools. But the gallery remained a critical space for you. It was where the conversations took place. Why is the gallery important and what possibilities do you see within this space that perhaps do not exist within others?

Garrett: Well, that's one of the things that we talked about. It was really looking at galleries in terms of what they should be for, and should they be, or are they, places of free expression? At one point I remember saying to you that, 'galleries are the last bastions of really true free expression', or at least that's what they should be considered as — open and democratic spaces. If an artist exhibits, they should be able to do and say exactly what they want to say and great curators are those that will facilitate that and allow that and encourage that. I think when I first started with radio and really got interested in it, I was really disappointed with what galleries were offering or doing at that time, but that was probably because I was working within a museum environment.

Contemporary art museums are very different to galleries in terms of the conversations that happen on ground level. But both galleries and museums can lose direction, can become very stoic and austere spaces, market-driven, sponsored, State-run and show non-confrontational work that's a little bit indulgent on the part of curators and artists. Many are heavily compromised for those reasons. I think we were being brave with *FREE THOUGHT FM*. We challenged the gallery, its situation and those around us and at a time when it needed to be done. We really went out of our way to find and engage and bring a new public into the space, which was a major priority for us. We went out of our way to say, 'you can have a real voice here and we can have a real conversation in this space' and I think that's what really interested me within what we were doing, as well as bringing those conversations into the grounds of Trinity College.

Georgina: Within your work there's a unique relationship between form and engagement. When you're thinking about what to make, what kind of a sculpture or whether or not to use radio, there's an urgency of thinking about what kind of engagement is possible with this medium. I remember walking through the streets of Dublin during *New Faith Love Song* where you had the church bells playing from St Patrick's and Christ Church Cathedral. And thinking about this song playing out from, and between, these imposing religious institutions,[8] institutions that have played such a critical role in Irish society, and the divisions that still exist. This idea of constantly thinking about engagement, who the audience is and how that audience comes into being, is clearly evident in *FREE THOUGHT FM*. Using a Broadcast Authority of Ireland licensed frequency, the station broadcast live on 105.2 FM, the same channel as Christmas FM. The idea of somebody scrolling through their radio in the car or on their phone and stumbling across a very different kind of conversation is so important. How do you think about the possibility of form and the consequences of engagement?

Garrett: Well firstly I have three conscious tiers of engagement. The first is 'ME', completely self-serving. I won't make anything that I don't want to make and what I do want to make has to be deeply personal because I know things can take a long time to realise and I know that if I make something deeply personal, I'm not going to lose my enthusiasm, I will remain totally committed to the project. The second is my peer group, the 'ART-WORLD' audience. These are people who might be able to experience and appraise my work a lot better than people who aren't familiar with the materials and platforms I use, but this is not always the case. My work demands time. The third audience is the 'ACCIDENTAL'. This goes back to the way I've developed my relationship with radio over the years since the early 90s. People would get in touch with me who had no relationship with the art world, they just came across the work. They are people who listen to radio at four in the morning, radio enthusiasts, people driving in their cars, insomniacs, those who work the late shift, parents of newborn children, all who occupy the twilight hours – there's always an alternative audience out there and that really interests me. I am very aware of that now and so I situate my works more purposefully with a public who might never engage with contemporary art. It's about finding new ways of communicating the same ideas.

I think my work reinvents the wheel in many respects. We are constantly faced with the same concerns, the same yearnings, the same loves, the same hates, the same banality, the difference each time being what we bring through our own experiences.

Georgina: Artist Isabel Nolan has argued that your works have "a magnitude and scope that is hard to describe". I think that's very visible within *FREE THOUGHT FM*. She continues, "we see an investigatory prowess at work that reveals the sort of truths that feel real – love can heal and forces physical, sonic, optical, mental and sensual can resonate through space and time and affect and connect us all".[9] Connection was a core part of this work, whether you're talking about the number of people involved, the many guests, those moments of kind of coming across the radio station and hearing these conversations. And one of the things that we talked about at length was the crucial role of care and compassion throughout the project. Why are these things so important to you?

Garrett: I agree with that – Isabel's put it politely in terms of 'magnitude' and 'scope' and 'hard to describe'. I layer things heavily because I spend a lot of time making things right. It's the same way an artist spends long periods of time building up clay on a maquette to arrive at a finished sculpture, small pieces of soft rolled clay and they start from the steel or wooden centre point and they build it up slowly but surely and then eventually it has form. That's a very simple metaphor but that is the way that I make these works, there is an anatomy to it. It is what it is once you experience it and no one knows that much about the history or the story behind how it has been arrived at. My practice, like you say, is really broad in terms of the materials or platforms I use and I've done that on purpose because I believe that certain mediums and certain platforms suit the content of the statement better than others. What might work well in photography would not work on radio.

In human psychology they say you need to give seven positive affirmations to disqualify one negative one. It is the human condition of negative bias. That really interests me. I think exploring the world of love and compassion and care is much more interesting to me than responding in a really aggressive angry way. With *New Faith Love Song*, which you mentioned, it was trying to contribute something culturally to the city that was having an appalling time in 2010 and 2011. The city was hurt, it was wounded, it was in bits economically. Financially, people were wiped out. What I wanted to do was create a symbol of care and support. Bells represent community for me. Ancient bells that have seen hard times and good times. So I created a simple conversation between two old towers using bells. A live, once-off performance. Basically what one tower was saying to the other tower was 'YOU WILL BE OK, I AM HERE FOR YOU'. As simple as that. It went on for 20 minutes, this bell ringing composition, which I wrote and worked on for many years with the bell ringers of both bell towers to try and understand how it could work as a conversation between two spaces. That was what I call a 'give back work'. A work for the city, a city that has given me so much. It rang out to the city in the midst of all the traffic and the noise, which is all part of the aural fabric of the city. It was a healing message.

Georgina: But then there is something more, which goes back to what you're saying about *New Faith Love Song*, that idea of healing the city. One of the other things that we talked about a lot when we were developing this project was that idea of being solutions-based. Let's not just talk about what all the problems are, let's look at how we can change things or how we can address these problems. It very specifically related to the marketing campaign with information on SUSI grants, talking about apprenticeships, talking about the CAO and when you can change your mind and the cost implications of that. All of this different information is being put out there to assist. And there is also a kind of care that emerges from the project that is not just an abstract idea – it's about how you worked with everybody who was part of the team, how you took care of them, how you were very considerate of people's welfare and mental health throughout the whole process and that extended from not only the team but to all of the guests that came in and everybody that you engaged with as part of this process, whether or not that was someone who DM'd you on Instagram or sent you a Facebook message. And I think that question of care, maybe it just goes back to this idea of connection, the community, the commons, all of these different terms that come up frequently in your work.

Garrett: I am not an artist whose career is dedicated to working with groups of people. I would not describe my practice as a participatory practice. Right now in life, as an artist, I am addressing issues that concern me at my age, as a partner, a son, a father, a friend, a citizen and I need to make my work and question my life in this way, creatively. At any point in time I can step out of this process quickly. My path as an artist is not dedicated to a specific form. With this in mind I have taken great care to ensure the work is executed properly and thoroughly. With art works like *FREE THOUGHT FM* I am responsible for the welfare of others throughout the course of the research/production and presentation. This can be overwhelming. The relationships can be overwhelming, as well as the outcomes. I think at the heart of these works is that I am trying to offer, suggest or present solutions.

Georgina: This leads me back to what your hopes were for *FREE THOUGHT FM* from the beginning point to the end point. I'm conscious that it's now almost two years since it happened.

Garrett: The project confirmed that class prejudice in Dublin is very much alive and it confirmed that successive governments have done virtually nothing to rectify the issue. Why this is the way it is becomes clearer when you listen to the voices and read the words of Liam Wegimont, Kathleen Lynch, Gerry Kearns and Ellen Rowley, on the *FREE THOUGHT FM* archive and in this book. *FREE THOUGHT FM* was about this question of why this inequality exists, and the truth of that can be found in the archive and in *HEED FM's* archive also. *FREE THOUGHT FM* was a very positive project as it fundamentally presented and illustrated a solution to the problem of accessing information on third-level education. We wanted to illustrate that there was a way in which you could disseminate important, life-changing information and make it more accessible. I think we certainly did that. We also have to think about what the end point is. Our actions were designed to support work already

being done to change the
understanding of class inequality
and access to education in
general through art, but also to
challenge the inequality and lack
of accessibility within our own
environment – the art world. We
weren't being critical of others
so much as being self-critical.
The questions we're asking of
the education system, we can
also ask of ourselves. So two
years later, we now publish this
book and distribute it for free and
make available these statements.
I hope this concludes the *FREE
THOUGHT FM* project by helping
its message to resonate that
little bit further, as a means to
encourage the creation of a freer
and more equal system for all.

Endnotes

1. *HEED FM* – Audio Archive is available at https://www.heedoffice.com/bandcamp-link.

2. Student Universal Support Ireland (SUSI) is Ireland's national awarding authority for all higher and further education grants. See https://susi.ie/.

3. The Disability Access Route to Education (DARE) is a third-level alternative admissions scheme for school leavers whose disabilities have had a negative impact on their second-level education. See http://accesscollege.ie/dare/.

4. The Higher Education Access Route (HEAR) is a college and university scheme that offers places on reduced points and extra college support to those who are resident in the Republic of Ireland and underrepresented at Higher Education due to their socio-economic background. See http://accesscollege.ie/hear/.

5. Ailbhe Smyth in conversation with Garrett Phelan. Available at: https://freethoughtfm.bandcamp.com/track/day-3-ailbhe-smyth.

6. McLuhan, M. (1964). Radio: The Tribal Drum. *Understanding Media: The Extensions of Man*. Sixth edition. New York: Signet (The New American Library), p. 263.

7. A.A.R.T. – Radio – Archive is available at https://aart-radio.bandcamp.com.

8. Christ Church was founded in the eleventh century and Saint Patrick's was founded in the twelfth century. Both medieval cathedrals are now Church of Ireland. The Roman Catholic Archdiocese of Dublin still recognises Christ Church as its seat, although Catholic liturgies have not been celebrated in either cathedral in almost five centuries.

9. Nolan, I. (2016). Garrett Phelan Has Seen Some Remarkable Things. See: http://www.thehideproject.com.

Garrett Phelan in conversation with Ailbhe Smyth

Garrett Phelan in conversation with Calvin D'arcy Kanda

Michelle Kinsella in conversation with John J. Ross

Garrett Phelan and Michelle Kinsella in conversation
with Martin Collins and Tamara Harawa

WALL 3

INSULATOR

CONDUIT

REMED

SOLVIT

DURACELL

REFLECTION

Members of The Irish Wheelchair Association, David Barry,
Kayleigh McKevitt and Rachel Creevy in conversation with
with Garrett Phelan, Michelle Kinsella and Tamara Harawa

Tamara Harawa in conversation with Henry Mkumbira Phiri

Brian Foley, Director of Ballymun Youth Action
Project in conversation with Sophie Mullervey

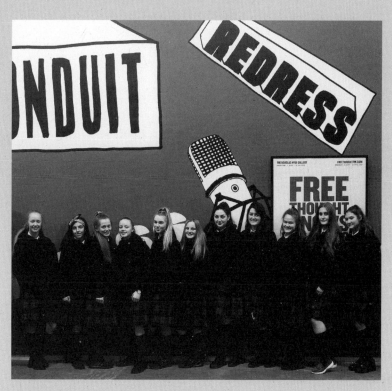

Students from Mercy Secondary School Inchicore

THOUGH

FM.CO

ACCESS AT ITS MOST ATTENTIVE, NOTES ON FREE THOUGHT FM

**It's about a class divide.
It's about third-level education
and structural inequality,
and ways of thinking that
disempower, dismiss and deny.**

**It's about a cultural divide.
It's about debt.**

**It's about the university and the gallery,
and ways of working that exclude,
delegitimate and disown.
It's about failure.**

On a Saturday afternoon in April 2019, I visit the Douglas Hyde in Trinity College, Dublin. I have already listened to *FREE THOUGHT FM* online via daily radio broadcasts that started after the exhibition opened. When I enter the gallery, the artwork is momentarily on hold, paused between scheduled sessions. Small talk, tidying up and other unmediated encounters fill the space. The exhibition design includes large-scale vinyl texts and drawings transferred directly onto the gallery walls, a microphone stand and mixer, and a number of soft, black pillows and folding chairs situated around the edges of the room.

FREE THOUGHT FM, like other artworks by Garrett Phelan, arrived after a long period of research and development. This aspect of Phelan's practice means that, from the onset, his role as artist includes oversight and administration, where his artistic ideas come into contact with a network of bureaucracies, organisations and vocational fields. In the case of *FREE THOUGHT FM*, a substantial amount of planning went into developing a publicity campaign with an Ireland-based marketing/PR company to announce the project and present information on access points to third-level education throughout Dublin city. Specifically, this information contains straightforward prose about how to apply for funding along with general details on the CAO application process. A considerable level of attention was paid to the language used in this pamphlet and the project's associated communications, with an aim to demystify Irish universities' admissions procedures and convey clear, understandable guidance.

The publicity campaign, conceived as part of the artwork, ran alongside the exhibition at the Douglas Hyde. Using public funding directly awarded to the artist to create new work, the resources allocated to this aspect of the project exceeded what is typically budgeted towards promotion for a solo exhibition at a contemporary space in Ireland. The underlying logic behind the publicity outlay speaks to a differential that arises in many public art projects between funds that support research, development and outreach, and funds that directly support artistic production. By realigning the project budget towards the former, more secondary aspects of the work and away from the primary activity of art-making, *FREE THOUGHT FM* raises questions about how public art is administered and disseminated, and what role advertising and promotion have in civic discourse. What if a social issue was afforded a substantive level of publicity attention? How might an artwork use the language of advertising to generate a public discussion?

Similar questions arose in the early development of *FREE THOUGHT FM*, driven by Phelan's growing concern over access to third-level education in Dublin and a class divide that makes admission prohibitive for some and impossible for many. No doubt the location of his solo exhibition at Trinity College, one of Ireland's most exclusive third-level institutions, in the equally prominent Douglas Hyde, underpinned Phelan's thinking to use the context of the university, the gallery and its infrastructure to focus on this particular issue. Over the course of the exhibition, Phelan and a project team that included Michelle Kinsella, Shane Brothwood, David Joyce, Sophie Mullervey, Calvin D'arcy Kanda and Tamara Halawa, hosted a series of conversations in the gallery space with over 150 invited contributors, identified by the artist as 'free thinkers'.

Drawn from a variety of backgrounds and ages, each guest brought a unique perspective on, and experience of, third-level education to the discussion. Most of the conversations were conducted casually as interviews, where Phelan asked his guests pointed questions about their personal understanding of education and class. Sometimes the discussion veered towards the abstract and speculative, offering Phelan and his interlocutors a chance to wonder about the value of higher learning, its social worth and its bearing on individual lives. In all of the conversations, there is an intimacy and degree of disclosure demonstrated by Phelan as a profound respect for the speaker's position, so that each day's programme becomes a kind of testimonial offered as part of a shared enquiry. The rambling, referential, parenthetical and anecdotal details usually held back in more formalised communications take precedence in *FREE THOUGHT FM* – they are intrinsic to what is happening.

As the show progressed, the talks were broadcast each day on 105.2FM and online. Those who visited the gallery could sit close by and listen, nestled into the conversation. Others wandered through the space at their own pace, while the rest of the world could tune in. This is how *FREE THOUGHT FM* summoned its audience. A daily occurrence, sequential, fractal, ritualised. To anyone who has experienced Phelan's radio-based projects, this openness to other ways of 'attending' is familiar. We tune in, alone and together, listening and projecting, spatially dislocated and temporally unbound.

The collected conversations are kept online at freethoughtfm.com, making *FREE THOUGHT FM*, the artwork, available in perpetuity. While it is not unusual for artworks to take place across different platforms, in *FREE THOUGHT FM* we enter a whole rubric of grammars, systems and structures that represent the work and affect how it behaves and is received – archive, exhibition, broadcast, publicity and information. *FREE THOUGHT FM* is all of this at once. The experiences that shape the work reshape and differentiate an experience of the work, according to its uses by a variegated public. From the sunken surrounds of the Douglas Hyde, against the backdrop of Trinity College, the work synchronises its parts into a cooperative whole, simultaneously reaching out, expanding and multiplying.

And yet, without exception, *FREE THOUGHT FM* situates itself from within these known, named places full of tradition and history, in the centre of a city marked by class, custom and contests of language (notable in the figure of Douglas Hyde himself). These locations register Phelan's keen understanding of everything this opportunity holds. A solo show at the Douglas Hyde gallery is a major accolade for any artist. A privileged moment. For artists in Ireland, it represents the top level of achievement and recognition, and the significance and weight of this occasion is not lost on Phelan. He uses it. With a singular focus and visibility afforded to the artist, Phelan brings the public in. Of prime concern are Phelan's guests and contributors, the speakers and free thinkers who enter the gallery for a conversation. Without falling into the trap of relational art which premises participation on the audience's engagement, *FREE THOUGHT FM* recedes in the presence of the gallery-goer. Indifferent and undisposed, the work is not there to be appreciated or activated; it is a backdrop to the main event.

If access is fundamentally and structurally about entering the university, then being inside matters. The conversations that populate *FREE THOUGHT FM* remind us of this. Access to third-level education is not simply about getting in — no one's story ends there. No experience of university concludes upon entry. On the contrary, access is experienced as an ongoing, embodied condition that adds up to more than the parts of an admissions process. The destinies of those who find a way into the university are not sealed by good fortune. Not by a long shot. Class comes into the equation, always, but in ways that are indeterminant and unexpected. What we learn from *FREE THOUGHT FM* is that access is structural and procedural on one hand, and provisional and internalised on the other. Improving access to third-level education is not just an administrative fix. Most universities understand this, with retention numbers a constant concern. Getting in is just the beginning.

After all, sustaining and valuing diverse, critical and inquisitive ways of working is the very basis of advanced study. If the university takes these values seriously, then lack of access to third-level education undermines them - completely. Access is not merely who's in and who's out. It is not about recognition or validation, or feeling indebted to the university. Access is how we enter the issues of our day, empowered and prepared. The student who has real, transformative access to everything university has to offer also knows what the university lacks. She brings her knowledge in and her expectations exceed its horizons.

In her seminal work, *Decolonizing Methodologies*,[1] Maori anthropologist Linda Tuhiwai Smith identifies ways of sharing knowledge where so-called anthropological 'subjects' actively inform research that is consensual, emergent and situated. Ethically, this is the opposite of research by observation and comparative study. If understood as an example of decolonising research, *FREE THOUGHT FM* attunes to class as a subject position that is held personally and cuts across categories like 'underprivileged' or 'working class' or 'immigrant'. Discursive practice as a means to learn from, not about, means no experience is disqualified or unquantifiable. Tuhiwai Smith calls particular attention to institutionalised practices rooted in colonial language, where words used over and over in the framework of the university reinforce colonial values. Research 'excavates', 'explores' and 'discovers'; knowledge is 'acquired' and subjects are 'conquered'.[2] Where research is hierarchical and exclusive, it rarely moves beyond the frame of the institution. By contrast, decolonising methodologies are neither external nor extracted, but rather they establish deep roots and operate collectively. This is a challenge to normative, prescribed indicators used to validate research from within. Access, as an indicator of equality, requires, first and foremost, acknowledging that research is not the exclusive domain of the university. Its contexts abound.

As I write, I am aware of current neoliberal tendencies in third-level education that transpose the language of capital onto the university. The student is a 'customer', knowledge is a 'deliverable' and teaching is a 'service'. The endless demands on research to 'produce outcomes' and 'measure impacts' has devastated the university's capacity to value, support and sustain attached, unconventional, and socially charged relationships and modalities as research. This radically changes the university's relationship to the student. Neoliberalism links success and failure to tuition payments, and time spent in the academy to professional pay-offs upon graduating. In this model, access is at odds with the flow of a free market; if neoliberalism thrives on individuation, neoliberal education thrives on individuals paying for it. The student goes into debt, and the university can't survive without her. The current paradigm in which the student finds herself is a tragic one.

Where do we go from here? If a portion of the population has no access to third-level education, it is not merely their 'loss'. Access is a measure of the university's solidarity with numerous life paths, embodiments, and struggles for visibility and justice. *FREE THOUGHT FM* stages this solidarity through the lens of personal experience and reclaims the university as part of the body politic. This raises the stakes of what it means to collect non-generalised responses to the topic of 'access'. Any insights are personal and not necessarily transferrable to all. The work fuses many disparate pathways without ever settling on 'the right path'. The issues are complex and multiply along with the many subjectivities at play.

Where neoliberalism works actively, persistently against us – against the very idea of 'us' – *FREE THOUGHT FM*'s methodology, worth recognising as such, calls upon energies that require sharing and support, calling forth and seeking out connective tissue and bringing it into the university, the gallery, the artwork. What better way to have a conversation about access than from inside? *FREE THOUGHT FM* raises the stakes of access as a form of embodied knowledge by placing responsibility for the enquiry on all of us. We are its agents. The artwork aligns a sense of the social, making itself available to anyone who needs it and utterly dependent upon those whose time, experiences and voices make up the archive. These urgencies carry the work. The aims are not about creating publics or forging new economies. The rhythms are more exacting, the concerns less totalising and consequential.

A constant refrain echoes through *FREE THOUGHT FM*, that there is more than one way. This plurality exhibited and bestowed, laid out in the very structure of the work, reveals access as a commitment to thinking and acting together. Taking time to appear, to reflect, to speak and to listen, *FREE THOUGHT FM* is access at its most attentive. It is the prioritisation of being with others in the depths of engagement.

Endnotes

1.   Tuhiwai Smith, L. (2012). *Decolonizing Methodologies: Research and Indigenous Peoples.* London: Zed Books.

2.   Ibid, p. 25.

APPENDIX

FREE THOUGHT FM —
ARCHIVE

To access the full
FREE THOUGHT FM – Archive visit
www.freethoughtfm.bandcamp.com

bandcamp   Search and discover music

music   community

Day 1 - Dr Georgina Jackson - The Douglas Hyde Gallery
/ in conversation with Garrett Phelan - 'FREE THOUGHT FM - Archive'

Da
/ in
Ph
- A

Day 1 - Ola Majekodunmi
/ in conversation with Garrett Phelan - 'FREE THOUGHT FM - Archive'

Da
In
/ in
Ph
'FI
Ar

Day 2 - Colleen Dube - Uversity
/ in conversation with Garrett Phelan and Michelle Kinsella - 'FREE THOUGHT FM - Archive'

Da
/ in
Ph
'FI
Ar

THOUGHT FM - ARCHIVE

FREE THOUGHT FM
Dublin, Ireland

Follow

Garrett Phelan is one
of Ireland's leading
visual artists who
continues to break
barriers of form and
engagement. Phelan
has... more

contact / help

Contact FREE
THOUGHT FM

Streaming and
Download help

Report this account

e Kinsella
with Garrett
HOUGHT FM

Day 1 - Andrea Horan
/ in conversation with Garrett
Phelan - 'FREE THOUGHT FM
- Archive'

**Day 1 - Daire Hennessy -
Citywise**
/ in conversation with Michelle
Kinsella - 'FREE THOUGHT
FM - Archive'

**agan - North
ore Project**
with Garrett
elle Kinsella -
FM -

Day 1 - Shane Brothwood
/ in conversation with Garrett
Phelan - 'FREE THOUGHT FM
- Archive'

**Day 2 - Liam Wegimont -
Mount Temple
Comprehensive School**
/ in conversation with Garrett
Phelan - 'FREE THOUGHT FM
- Archive'

osgrave
with Garrett
elle Kinsella -
FM -

**Day 2 - Professor Christine
Casey - TCD**
/ in conversation with Garrett
Phelan - 'FREE THOUGHT FM
- Archive'

**Day 2 - Tammy Darcy - The
Shona Project**
/ in conversation with Garrett
Phelan and Michelle Kinsella -
'FREE THOUGHT FM -
Archive'

CONTRIBUTOR BIOGRAPHIES

Georgina Jackson is the Director of the Douglas Hyde Gallery of Contemporary Art at Trinity College Dublin. She was previously the Director of Exhibitions + Programs at Mercer Union, a centre for contemporary art in Toronto where she commissioned new work by artists including Deanna Bowen, Duane Linklater and Carlos Motta. She completed her curatorial-practice based PhD, exploring how large-scale international exhibitions have been increasingly posited as a space for the *political*, through the Graduate School of Creative Arts and Media, Dublin. Prior to this she was the Exhibitions Curator at Dublin City Gallery The Hugh Lane, Project Curator at the Irish Museum of Modern Art and Curator-in-Residence at The Mattress Factory art museum in Pittsburgh. She has taught at the National College of Art and Design, the Institute of Art, Design and Technology, Dun Laoghaire, TU Dublin, and the University of Toronto. She also contributes to art journals, most recently *Afterall*. She is a member of the Steering Committee of the National Campaign for the Arts.

Gerry Kearns is Professor of Geography at Maynooth University, member of the Maynooth University Social Sciences Institute and a member of the Royal Irish Academy. His research is at the intersection of political, health and historical geographies and he is the author of *Geopolitics and Empire: The Legacy of Halford Mackinder* (Oxford University Press, 2009; winner of the Murchison Award of the Royal Geographical Society 2010) and co-editor, with David Meredith and John Morrissey, of *Spatial Justice and the Irish Crisis* (Royal Irish Academy, 2014). At Maynooth he teaches on the undergraduate degree in Geography and on the Masters in Spatial Justice. With Nessa Cronin and Karen Till, he is a director of the earthwritings.ie project. His work on geography and art may be accessed at geographicalturn.wordpress.com. He is currently working on *Plague and Providence: Making Space for AIDS*, a study of cultural activism during the AIDS epidemic.

Kathleen Lynch is Professor Emerita of Equality Studies at University College Dublin (UCD), and a Professor in the School of Education. Her teaching and research are guided by the belief that the purpose of scholarship and research is not just to understand the world but to change it for the good of all humanity. She has worked over many years to promote equality and social justice through education, research and activism. She was appointed as a Commissioner of the Irish Equality and Human Rights Commission in 2020. Kathleen played a leading role in establishing the UCD Equality Studies Centre and the UCD School of Social Justice. She has published extensively on equality and education issues throughout her life, and more recently on issues of affective equality, care and social justice. Her recent co-authored books include *New Managerialism in Education: Commercialisation, Carelessness and Gender* (2012, 2015) and *Affective Equality: Love, Care and Injustice* (2009). Her forthcoming book *Care and Capitalism* will be published by Polity Press, Cambridge in December 2021.

Dr Rachel O'Dwyer is a Lecturer in Digital Cultures in the School of Visual Cultures in the National College of Art and Design, Dublin and the institution's acting Fulbright Ambassador. She is a research fellow in the OMG group in Connect, Trinity College Dublin, the Science Foundation Ireland centre for future networks and telecommunications, and a former IRC Government of Ireland postgraduate research fellow. She writes about topics including surveillance capitalism, digital money, algorithms and ethics, online activism, and media art, most recently for publications including *UnDark Magazine, LongReads, The London Review of Books* and *Circa*. She regularly curates events on these topics, including the Dublin Art and Technology Association (2009-2017) and the Openhere festival. She is a co-editor of *Neural, critical digital culture and media arts* and the founding editor in chief of *Interference, a journal of audio culture* (2009-2017). She is currently completing a book on the political economy of radio and wireless activism. She lives in Sligo with her husband Patrick and son Ted.

Since 2003 **Sarah Pierce** has used the term The Metropolitan Complex to describe her project, characterised by forms of gathering, both historical examples and those she initiates. The processes of research and presentation that Pierce undertakes demonstrate a broad understanding of cultural work and a continual renegotiation of the terms for making art, the potential for dissent, and self-determination. Pierce works with installation, performance, archives, talks and papers, often opening these up to the personal and the incidental in ways that challenge received histories and accepted forms. Her interests include radical pedagogies and student work, art historical legacies and figures such as El Lissitzky, August Rodin, and Eva Hesse, and theories of community and love founded in Maurice Blanchot and Georges Bataille. She is based in Dublin where she teaches in the School of Visual Culture at the National College of Art and Design.

Garrett Phelan's distinctive practice is manifested through ambitious projects including independent FM radio broadcasts, sculptural installations, drawing installations, photography, animations, zines and text ephemera. In recent years he has completed a series of large-scale ambitious projects that respond to specific issues within our society. In 2016 he created *HEED FM*, a 28-day anonymous broadcast sound portrait of 18–25 year olds from all backgrounds living in Dublin, a generation whose opinions and beliefs are rarely heard in the public realm. The archive for *HEED FM* can be found on Bandcamp. More recently, he has realised *THE HIDE PROJECT*, commissioned by Fingal County Council as a permanent functional public art work that is continually shaped by its role as a shared space for reflection and creative actions. Information on this can be found at www.thehideproject.com

Ellen Rowley is Assistant Professor in Modern Irish Architecture in the School of Architecture (APEP) at University College Dublin. She mostly thinks about and writes on Irish architectural Modernism, including her history of Dublin housing *Housing, Architecture and the Edge Condition* (Routledge, 2019) and the series *More than Concrete Blocks*, 1900–40 (Vol. 1, 2016), 1940–72 (Vol. 2, 2019), of which Volume 3 (1973–2000) is forthcoming. As well as teaching and researching, Ellen is committed to public engagement, curating Dublin's tenement museum (14 Henrietta Street, 2016–18), UCD's 50 year architectural history 'Belfield 50' (2020) and a radio series on housing and home (Davis Now lectures, Raidió Teilifís Éireann, 2019–20).

Liam Wegimont is Executive Director of GENE – Global Education Network Europe – the European network Ministries and Agencies with national responsibility for Global Education in European countries. Since 2005, he has been the principal of Mount Temple Comprehensive School, a school on the northside of Dublin with the motto: All Different, All Equal. He is currently on secondment to GENE. Liam has been involved in education for social change, local and global, and in formal and non-formal education for over 30 years – as a teacher, youth worker, teacher-educator, school principal, curriculum developer, evaluator and speaker. Liam co-founded GENE (www.gene.eu) and more recently co-initiated ANGEL – the Academic Network on Global Education Learning. (www.angel-network.net). He is a member of the editorial board of the International Journal of Development Education and Global Learning Institute of Education, UCL, London and of Sinergias ED, CEAUP, Oporto, and has been Visiting Lecturer in Teacher Education and Global Learning at Friedrich-Alexander-Universität Erlangen-Nürnberg and Trinity College Dublin.

THANK YOU *FREE THOUGHT FM* **was realised through the work of many individuals, collaborators and organisations, over the weeks of the exhibition itself, and the years of preparation leading up to it. We would like to take this opportunity to thank all those that have been instrumental in the making of** *FREE THOUGHT FM.*

This project would not have happened without the support and belief of the Arts Council / An Chomhairle Ealaíon through the *Making Great Art Work – Open Call* **award (2018), an initiative which funds ambitious, one-off artistic projects by some of Ireland's best artists and arts organisations.**

Garrett Phelan would like to thank:

Dr Georgina Jackson, Director of the Douglas Hyde, for the invitation and for her immense support and collaboration throughout the project; the Douglas Hyde team that worked on the project: Olen Bajarias, Sophie Behal, Rachel Donnelly, Isadora Epstein, Eoghan McIntyre, Rachel McIntyre, Blaine O'Donnell, Cliodhna O'Riordan, Eimear Regan, Joe Scullion and Aideen Quirke; the *FREE THOUGHT FM* team: Michelle Kinsella (Project Coordinator), Shane Brothwood, Calvin D'arcy Kanda, Tamara Harawa, David Joyce and Sophie Mullervey; the Broadcasting Authority of Ireland; Joe King, and the staff of Broadcast Technical Services; the team at Thinkhouse, especially, Jane Mc Daid, David Coyle, David Balfe, Stephen Kenny, Laura King, Siobhan Brosnan, Amber Wilson and Donna Parsons; Tom Pawlik and Donna Cox from Inksplash, Mary Byrne from Irish Poster Advertising Ltd, and Dr Lisa

Godson. In particular, Garrett would like to thank Sarah Glennie for her unwavering understanding and patience, Finola Mc Ternan, Liam Wegimont for their important encouragement and support for the project, and Michelle Kinsella who, as always, was an incredible brain, support and sounding board. Noelle Cooper and all at Unthink for their creative collaboration on the making of this book.

A huge thank to you to each of the *FREE THOUGHT FM* contributors:

Day 1: Dr Georgina Jackson (Director, The Douglas Hyde); Michelle Kinsella (Associate Lecturer, Adult and Community Education, Maynooth University; Learning Specialist for Design + Innovation, Irish Management Institute); Andrea Horan (Founder, HunReal Issues; owner, Tropical Popical; Co-Founder, United Ireland Podcast); Daire Hennessy (Development Officer, Citywise Education); Ola Majekodunmi (presenter, *Comhrá le Ola*; researcher, RTÉ 2FM; presenter, Raidió na Life 106.4FM); Terry Fagan (North Inner City Folklore Project); Shane Brothwood (team member, *FREE THOUGHT FM*).

Day 2: Liam Wegimont (Principal, Mount Temple Comprehensive School; Executive Director, Global Education Network Europe (GENE)); Colleen Dube (CEO, National Adult Literacy Agency (NALA); CEO, Uversity); Anna Cosgrave (Founder, Repeal Project); Professor Christine Casey (Professor, Department of History of Art and Architecture, Trinity College Dublin); Tammy Darcy (CEO, The Shona Project; CEO, Social Enterprise ROI); Daniel McFarlane (Transition Year Project Officer, Trinity Access Programmes); Diane McSweeney (Senior Cycle School Coordinator, Trinity Access Programmes); Dr Lucy Michael (Lecturer,

Ulster University School of Applied Social and Policy Sciences; President, Sociological Association of Ireland).

Day 3: Ailbhe Smyth (Irish academic, feminist and LGBTQ activist); Martin Collins (Co-Director, Pavee Point Traveller + Roma Centre); David Barry, Kayleigh McKevitt, Rachel Creevy (members of the Irish Wheelchair Association); Spekulativ Fiktion (Irish musician); Chris Beausang (Doctoral Candidate, Maynooth University Arts and Humanities Institute).

Day 4: Lucy Masterson (CEO, Irish Youth Foundation); Professor Gerry Kearns (Head of Geography Department, Maynooth University); Aisling Moore (singer, songwriter); Maeve Stone (freelance theatre director, composer, writer); David Joyce (team member, *FREE THOUGHT FM*); John J. Ross (HDip Graduate, Further Education, Maynooth University); Aideen Quirke (formerly Assistant Curator, Douglas Hyde Gallery, now Director, Cork Printmakers).

Day 5: Shane Keeling (Bad Man Ceramics, artist); Maria Connor and Monica Caulfield (University College Dublin Access Graduates); Calvin D'arcy Kanda (team member, *FREE THOUGHT FM*); Jamie Mangan, SUBSET (artist collective).

Day 6: *Seen – Unseen* art project (a group exploring creative and cultural experiences with visually impaired collaborators); MathMan (Irish rapper, music producer); Jane Fogarty (artist); Marcus Joule (IT Helpdesk Support Lead at Brown Thomas, Arnotts); Henry Mkumbira Phiri (international student); Dr Camilla Fitzsimons (Lecturer, Adult and Community Education, Maynooth University).

Day 8: Amy Smith (Dyslexia Association Ireland); Donald Ewing (Head of Psychological and Educational Services at Dyslexia Association of Ireland (DAI)); Fergus Kelly (artist); Shane Brothwood (team member, *FREE THOUGHT FM*); Karen Horan (National Administrator, National Advocacy Service for People with Disabilities).

Day 9: Carmel O'Connor (Manager, St Andrews Resource Centre); Shane Mc Kenna (Director Dabbledoo Music, musician, music educator); Mercy Secondary School Inchicore; Sophie Mullervey (team member, *FREE THOUGHT FM*); Francis Conway.

Day 10: Eimear Regan (artist, performer); Phelim O Laoghaire / Sean Pierson (previous members, TCD Metafizz Society); Leanne Joyce (UCD Access Graduate); Charlotte Byrne (Education Officer, Irish Refugee Council); Lesley Keegan (School Completion Programme Coordinator, The Ballyfermot A School Completion Programme); Aoife Dooley (illustrator, author, comedian); Oein DeBhairduin (writer; Manager, Clondalkin Travellers Training Centre).

Day 11: Dr Katriona O'Sullivan (Lecturer, Department of Psychology and Researcher, Assisting Living + Learning Institute, Maynooth University); Baz Hickey (DJ); Sibyl Montague (artist); Dr Rory Mc Daid (Head of Department of Policy and Practice, Marino Institute of Education); young people from St Andrews Resource Centre; Mark MacMathúna and Eoghan Connolly (Trinity Access Programme Students).

Day 12: Professor Lorraine Leeson (Professor, Deaf Studies at the Centre for Deaf Studies Trinity College Dublin); Mary Broe (PhD Student, Geography Department, Maynooth University); Declan Meenagh (Councillor, Labour Party); Dr Bríd Connolly (Lecturer,

Adult and Community Education Department, Maynooth University); Diego Albuck (writer, actor); Dr Lucy Michael (CEO, Irish Youth Foundation).

Day 13: John Cunningham (Commercial Director, Morgan McKinley Group; CEO People Dynamic Solutions LTD; Director, CheckRisk LLP; Senior Advisor, Ireland INC; Board Member, IMMA; Chair of Gaisce, The President's Award); Conor Murray (Trinity College Dublin Graduate); Rory Chester; Michael McDonagh.

Day 15: Dr Cliona Hannon (Director, Trinity Access Programmes); Conor Lucey (Lecturer, Assistant Professor, School of Art History and Cultural Policy, University College Dublin); Joe Geary (Trainee Counselling Psychologist); Ross Malervy (General Manager, Social and Political Review (SPR)); Shubhangi Karmakar (Reviewer, Journal of Medical Ethics (BMJ); Editor-in-Chief, Trinity Student Scientific Review); Éilis Ryan (Councillor, The Workers' Party of Ireland).

Day 16: Dr Maire Ní Mhórdha (Social Anthropologist, Maynooth University); Joyce Gough (Adult Literacy Organiser) and pre-college course group from Parnell Adult Learning Centre; Declan Markey (Community Outreach, Maynooth University); TU Dublin 4th Year Fine Art Students; Lynn Whelan; Dr Orla Lehane (Education Director, Fighting Words).

Day 17: Francesco Sani (music lecturer, Edinburgh College); Fiona Whelan (socially engaged artist, Rialto Youth Project); Crumlin Youthreach; Noel Smith and Angie Hart (Youth Workers, SWAN Youth Service, Dublin); Jesse Presley Jones (artist) and Donna Rose (Fellow, ESB Centre for the Study of Irish Art).

Day 18: Pre-college course

group from Parnell Adult Learning Centre; Eibhlín Harrington and Niamh Molloy (SWAN Youth Service); Clare Seoighe (Dublin College University Graduate); Jobst Graeve (curator); Desmond Aston (National and Schools Coordinator, Trinity College Dublin Centre for People with Intellectual Disabilities); Heidi Dwyer (secondary school art teacher, artist).

Day 19: Martina Flynn (JCSP Librarian, St. Aidan's Community School, Tallaght); Scott Boylan and Lucy Lloduba (students, WraPParound); Paul Uzell (Community Activist); Sophie Murphy; Ciaran Kirwan (secondary school art teacher, artist); Anne-Marie Collins.

Day 20: Brian Foley (Lead Trainer, Motivational Interviewing Training, Ireland; Chairperson, Ballymun Recovery); Davie Chibvvana (hip-hop artist); Elayne Harrington (artist; (AKA) Temper-Mental MissElayneous).

Day 22: David Frew (secondary school teacher, musician); David Joyce (solicitor, human rights activist); Finola McTernan (Access Officer, National College of Art and Design); Jen Liston and Ann Devitt (Assistant Professors, School of Education, Trinity College Dublin); Claire Seoighe and Ronan Mulligan (Dublin College University graduates).

Day 23: Elva O'Callaghan (Yellow Flag Coordinator); Emmet Kirwan (actor, playwright, screenwriter); Jenny Byrne (Information Officer, Dyslexia Association of Ireland (DAI)); Adrian Duncan (artist, author); Sé Merry Doyle (filmmaker); Rachael Melvin (artist); Alex Mc Dermott (artist).

Day 24: Jeanette Lowe (photographic artist); Brian Kirwan (Social Inclusion Manager, Dublin North Inner City and County), Professor Kathleen Lynch (Professor, Equality Studies, University

College Dublin); Dr Derek Barter (Coordinator, Continuing Education Programmes and Manager, BA Local Studies and BA Community Studies, Maynooth University); Shaz Oye (Previous President, Graduate Students' Union (GSU), University College Dublin).

Day 25: Dr Ellen Rowley (Lecturer / Assistant Professor, School of Architecture, Planning and Environmental Policy, University College Dublin); Mairéad McDevitt (Community Work Lead, Migrant Rights Centre Ireland); Catherine Whelan (independent business mentor, facilitator professional) and Shane Meehan (Enterprise Development Managers, Inner City Enterprise); Dr Stephen Lucek (Postdoctoral Fellow, Linguistics, University College Dublin); Amanda Coogan (artist); Professor Linda Doyle (Formerly Vice President for Research / Dean of Research, Professor of Engineering and The Arts, Trinity College Dublin, now Provost).

Day 26: Austin Magee (commercial pilot); Declan Clarke (visiting teacher, Travellers for North-East Dublin City) and David Joyce (team member, *FREE THOUGHT FM*); Liam Ó Maonlaí (musician); Ruth Maxwell (curator of *Not Consent* exhibition).

Day 27: Ray Hegarty (lens-based socially engaged artist); Maïa Nunes (performer, artist) and Karen Miano (DJ, writer, Founder of Origins Eile, DIAxDEM); Dr Tina Kinsella (Head of Department of Design + Visual Arts, IADT); Anthony Burrowes (Member Engagement Manager, Cooperative Housing Ireland); John White (musician, music teacher, SWAN Youth Services); Brian Maguire (artist).

Day 30: Female Empowerment Group Cabinteely Community School; Dr Francis Halsall (Lecturer, History/Theory of Modern and Contemporary Art,

National College of Art and Design); Owen Boss (Co-Artistic Director, ANU Productions); Austin Campbell, Ronya Phoenix and Eddie Dooner (My Streets Ireland); Christy Woods (sociology teacher, Pathways Centre); Shane Brothwood, Eoghan McIntyre, David Joyce, Tamara Harawa, Sophie Mullervey (team members, *FREE THOUGHT FM*); Dr Georgina Jackson (Director, The Douglas Hyde Gallery).

Speakers at the opening of *FREE THOUGHT FM* on 14 March 2019: Temper-Mental MissElayneous, Shubhangi Karmakar and Garrett Phelan.

Speakers at the *FREE THOUGHT FM* offsite school talks series: Aoife Dooley, Shaun Dunne, Temper-Mental MissElayneous, Katriona and John O'Sullivan, and Emmet Kirwan.

COLOPHON

Published by Garrett Phelan and the Douglas Hyde Gallery of Contemporary Art as part of Garrett Phelan, *FREE THOUGHT FM*, presented in Gallery 1 of the Douglas Hyde from Friday 15 March 2017 until Saturday 25 May 2019, and broadcast live from the gallery from Monday 25 March until Tuesday 23 April 2019 on 105.2FM (Greater Dublin area only), and nationally/internationally online at www.freethoughtfm.com.

FREE THOUGHT FM was generously supported through The Arts Council / *An Chomhairle Ealaíon's Making Great Art Work – Open Call* award, an Arts Council initiative which funds ambitious, one-off artistic projects by some of Ireland's best artists and arts organisations.

Editors
Georgina Jackson and Garrett Phelan

Copy Editing
Rachel Donnelly

Editorial Assistant
Rachel Botha

Design
Unthink

Printing
Impress

Cover drawing, *Nurture* (2021), page 6, Cover of *FREE THOUGHT FM ZINE* (2019), and pages 30/31, 84/85, 128/129, 144/145, *Studies for FREE THOUGHT FM* (2019), all by Garrett Phelan.

Photographs on pages 126/127 and 130/131 by the *FREE THOUGHT FM* team. All other photography by Louis Haugh, unless otherwise noted.

Garrett Phelan
www.garrettphelan.com

The Douglas Hyde Gallery of Contemporary Art
Trinity College, Dublin 2, Ireland
www.douglashyde.ie

The Douglas Hyde Gallery of Contemporary Art is supported by the Arts Council/ An Chomhairle Ealaíon and Trinity College Dublin.

ISBN: 978-1-905397-69-3

Trinity College Dublin
Coláiste na Tríonóide, Baile Átha Cliath
The University of Dublin